WRITING & PUBLIS

How To Books on Successful Writing

Copyright & Law for Writers
Creating a Twist in the Tale
Creative Writing
How to Be a Freelance Journalist
How to Master Business English
How to Publish a Book
How to Publish a Newsletter
How to Start Word Processing
How to Write a Press Release
How to Write a Report
How to Write an Assignment
How to Write an Essay
How to Write & Sell Computer
  Software
How to Write Business Letters
How to Write for Publication
How to Write for Television
How to Write Your Dissertation
Improving Your Written English
Mastering Business English
Writing a Nonfiction Book
Writing an Essay
Writing & Publishing Poetry
Starting to Write
Writing & Selling a Novel
Writing & Selling Short Stories

Other titles in preparation

The How To Series now contains more than 200 titles in the following categories:

Business Basics
Family Reference
Jobs & Careers
Living & Working Abroad
Student Handbooks
Successful Writing

Please send for a free copy of the latest catalogue for full details (see back cover for address).

SUCCESSFUL WRITING

WRITING & PUBLISHING POETRY

How to develop your creative
work for publication

Stephen Wade

How To Books

By the same author
Studying for a Degree: How to succeed as a mature student in higher education

Cartoons by Mike Flanagan

British Library Cataloguing in Publication Data
A catalogue record for this book is available from the British Library.

First published in 1997 by How To Books Ltd, 3 Newtec Place,
Magdalen Road, Oxford OX4 1RE, United Kingdom.
Tel: (01865) 793806. Fax: (01865) 248780.

Note: The material contained in this book is set out in good faith for
general guidance and no liability can be accepted for loss or expense
incurred as a result of relying in particular circumstances on statements
made in the book. The laws and regulations are complex and liable to
change, and readers should check the current position with the relevant
authorities before making personal arrangements.

Produced for How To Books by Deer Park Productions.
Typeset by Concept Communications (Design & Print) Ltd, Crayford, Kent.
Printed and bound by Cromwell Press, Broughton Gifford, Melksham, Wiltshire.

Contents

List of Illustrations

Preface

There are several useful books available about understanding poetry, and also some concerned with the technicalities of writing poetry in great detail. This book intends to provide you with a unique mix: an account of the basic skills involved but also some advice about how your poetry could get into print. It has been written with the beginner and the enthusiast in mind.

There are two main reasons why this book is unique. First, it is written in a way that avoids critical jargon wherever possible, so cutting out the usual clouds of abstraction that wrap a certain mystique about the art of poetry. Second, it aims to show that poetry is undergoing a quiet revolution in our culture, and if you want to be a part of that, then this is for you.

The images of starving poet in the garret and egoist spouting indulgent verse have gone. Poetry is now a thriving, vibrant accessible artform and poets have important and pressing things to say to us in our fast-changing world.

If you are a part-time writer or a student just confronting the classic poets, or if you already write in other forms or genres, it doesn't matter. This book is still for you. It is an exciting time to be writing poetry, and I know that this short introduction will provide you with tools to do the job, provided that you bring your imagination and experience of life to bear on the task.

Stephen Wade

IS THIS YOU?

Accounts clerk   Machine operative

Teacher

Solicitor   Secretary

Computer operator

Driver   Mechanic

Student

Houseperson   Bar staff

Accountant

Postman   Retailer

Retired professional

Salesperson   Representative

Journalist

Armed forces member   Businessperson

Labourer

Delivery worker   Grocer

Taxi driver

Hotel manager   Police officer

Surveyor

Plumber   Sales assistant   Warehouse worker

All these people entered competitions last
year and write for pleasure.

1
Getting Started

KNOWING THE BUSINESS OF WRITING

Poetry is tremendously popular now. That may be an astounding fact to many people, particularly as poetry in our culture has a negative image. After all, for many years we were subjected to the indignity of having to memorise long narrative poems for school recitals. The very word 'Shakespeare' could suggest boredom and having to virtually translate his poetry into modern, plain English. The media have not helped, either. Poets are often depicted as being effete, out of touch with reality, concerned with images of roses and swans, using an artificial language.

But all this has changed. Now, thousands of people of all ages are writing poetry. There are poetry competitions almost every week and the two most prestigious ones, organised by the *Observer* and by the Poetry Society, attract thousands of entrants. We now have so many forms of poetry. There is performance poetry, concrete poetry, pop lyric, dramatic verse, poetry written in dialect and slang and so on. The cliché of the art for art's sake, do your own thing, has gone, except in the most backward-looking contexts.

Being professional
The fact is, if you want to write poetry for publication, then you're going to find some stiff opposition, so you need a professional attitude from the start. What does this mean? For any type of writing, the word professional implies:

- a serious attitude to the skills needed
- a commitment to acquiring a body of knowledge
- an openness to learning from others
- an acceptance of high standards
- a willingness to learn slowly and take advice
- knowledge of the importance of good quality submissions.

There is a lot to learn, but this professional attitude means that you create a good impression on other professionals such as editors and publishers. It is a state of mind, an attitude, that accepts only the best of which you are capable.

You need to consider why you have chosen to write poetry. To many, it is the one form of writing that enables you to write about anything in any form possible. The idea of 'contemplating your navel' and writing spontaneously is a myth that refuses to go away. In reality, the poets who have achieved respect and a good status have had something to write about – a **theme**. A close reading of a poet's work from early juvenilia to mature writings will reveal that there are certain driving forces, constant preoccupations in the mind, which have been examined and explored from different angles. In other words, the best poetry grows naturally out of personality.

UNDERSTANDING POETRY TODAY

Contemporary poetry deals very much with the way we live: the effects of social change, political power, the impact of feminism, the collapse of Communism, what it feels like to live in an inner city and so on. Poetry has always been an art that both monitors today and provides visions of a possible future.

In the past, there have been firm conventions about what language should be used in a poem or what form the poem should take, but now, there are different ideas. For instance, in the sixties, folk music and social protest songs could be read and listened to for the strength of their lyrics. Bob Dylan, Leonard Cohen, Simon and Garfunkel and many more wrote lyrics which could be studied and reflected on just as much as traditional 'page' poetry. Poetry now involves almost every use of language that is possible in our culture. London poet Benjamin Zephaniah whose most well-known collection is *City Psalms*, writes in patois; the regional poets use dialect; many writers consciously challenge the standard English that has defined the nature of poetry for centuries.

A voice of protest?

Poetry, then, has grit. It is an art that confronts a society facing a frightening rate of change, revolutionary technology and a challenge to the individual in what many have called a postmodern world: one which shifts meanings almost daily. Like graffiti, poetry has always been a small voice of commentary or protest somewhere in a community, often anonymous and often reviled. But there is an influence. Percy Bysshe Shelley (1792–1822) said that 'Poets are the unacknowledged legislators of the world'; another poet, when asked whether poetry could change the world, replied that it changes people, and people can change the world!

How do you take steps to understand all this, so that your poetry can be a part of this, and speak as a meaningful contemporary voice? You could do some of the following things:

● Read poetry in magazines and books.

● Join an organisation such as the Poetry Society.

● Join local writing groups and learn from experienced writers.

● Read and listen to statements about poetry in the media.

● Do a course in English literature and learn about poetic form.

● Read the creative writing magazines.

LEARNING FROM HISTORY

Poets need to know the main ideas of poets from the past. There is a great deal of formal poetry in the body of English literature. The so-called canon – the classic, established texts such as John Milton, William Wordsworth and Alfred Lord Tennyson – will soon demonstrate that for centuries, most English poets wrote according to rules and guidelines that relate to those obeyed by the Greek and Latin poets. The study of classics in our culture meant that the art of poetry was learned in a grammar school, with students copying the verse forms of the poets of classical civilisation. When the Latin grammar had been well absorbed, the scholar translated, say, a satire from Juvenal or an ode of Horace. The great English poets of the canon would all know the metre, conventions of rhyme and accepted diction (or vocabulary) of poetry. For instance, it would be impossible to write a poem in a local dialect unless this was an experimental or curiosity item, such as Tennyson's two poems on Lincolnshire farmers, *The Northern Farmer Old Style* and *The Northern Farmer New Style*.

There were rules of technique, a sort of decorum or good manners of poetry writing that was part of an unwritten law for aspiring poets. For instance, many people still define poetry as rhymed lines in a certain pattern. Traditionally, poets would write poems in lines or stanzas (sections of a poem) with a pattern of end-rhymes. It was only in the early years of this century that these conventions were widely challenged.

THE CASE OF MODERNISM

In the Great War (1914–18) Wilfred Owen wrote about the ordinary soldiers in the trenches. Although he was an officer, had been to grammar school and knew all about the poetry of John Keats and the classics, he knew that to write about 'Tommy Atkins' he would have to use their language. Where the classes rubbed shoulders, so did the stylised poetic language meet the colloquial. Owen has these lines which describe a gas attack, for instance:

> Gas! Gas! Quick, boys! – An ecstasy of fumbling,
> Fitting the clumsy helmets just in time;
> But someone still was yelling out and stumbling . . .
> (*Dulce et Decorum Est*)

Although he still uses rhyme, it is a different way of describing, with new types of words and syntax. **Modernism** is the name given to much of the writing in the first twenty years of this century, and what characterised this was a drive to innovate, to try new forms and to write about all areas of experience, across the class-divides in our society. Much of this is still an influence now.

Question
Do I have to know all this background knowledge about the history of poetry just so I can start to write?

Answer
Not at all. This simply adds some depth to what you do, just as all artists find that it helps to be aware of what has been done by the best people in their field.

FINDING YOUR MATERIAL

So what do you write about? In a sense, the question is absurd. Poets

usually start to write from some emotional need, as opposed to nov-
elists who learn a 'trade' – or, at least, that is the conventional view.
But is that right? Why can't poetry be learned as a craft, just as writing a story or a radio script can? If poetry can be a commentary on
one's times and contemporaries, then surely, you can learn the
techniques?

There are several questions here that need to be asked about
yourself.

● Do you find yourself drawn to particular poets?

● Have your first attempts at writing been almost copies?

● Do you tend to be drawn to writing with rhyme?

● Do you enjoy the discipline of a formal poem?

● Can you explain the difference between verse and prose?

These questions are intended to make you think about what sort of
personality, approach and preferences go into what you have tried to
write already or into what you might produce. For instance, many
poets are drawn to writing poetry after reading a poet they personally find inspirational. In the sixties, when Pop Poetry appeared, and
was made popular by the Mersey Poets, Roger McGough, Brian
Patten and Adrian Henri, students in their thousands wrote short
lyrics for college magazines using the humour, idiom and forms of
that Mersey poetry.

There is nothing wrong with this. Most writers have had 'model'
writers who have influenced them. In fact, it can only be beneficial,
as it gives you the confidence to search for your particular difference,
your individual voice.

Two views of poetry

You might consider these two pieces of poetry, both written in the
eighteenth century. First, Alexander Pope (1688–1744):

> Presume not heaven to scan
> The proper study of mankind is man.
> *(An Essay on Man II)*

Then Thomas Gray:

> The curfew tolls the knell of parting day,
> The lowing herd winds slowly o'er the lea.
> The ploughman homeward plods his weary way,
> And leaves the world to darkness and to me.
>   (*Elegy written in a Country Churchyard*)

Pope's words give a general, philosophic reflection on life. They are an abstract thought about thinking. Gray's words describe a scene and a mood. He himself is present in the lines, unlike Pope.

This is a very simple point, but it shows two broad approaches to writing poetry. One depends on the poet and the mood, place and feeling. The other is detached; it stands back, distant but still a voice of thinking and commenting on the world. Which is naturally you? You need to ask basic questions about yourself before writing to themes or to techniques.

A lot of this concerns *your temperament*. For instance, if you have a sense of humour, are outgoing and lively, with a wry sense of the bizarre and absurd, you might write for performance or readings – or even for broadcast. If you tend to be the reflective type, interested in thought and feeling, then you may write solely for the page – for magazines initially perhaps, or for anthologies.

LEARNING BY READING

All writers should read. Talk to virtually any successful writer and they will have favourite authors. Only by reading and then analysing your responses to what you have read, will you make progress. If you are really serious about writing poetry, examine the reasons why you have chosen it. Most people write poetry because they have a deep emotion to put into words. A sailor in the last war, told me that he wrote just one poem in his life. It was never printed, but it went as follows:

> Although with every minute I am sailing far away,
> You know I always think of you, each minute of the day.

And he never wrote anything else in rhyme. Many people are like this. They need the form of poetry in certain places, or on occasions such as bereavement or parting. Poetry is related to religious and philosophical feelings, but a real poet will be able to write on subjects and feelings far more diverse than these occasional settings. In other words, ask yourself why you read what you read and find out what it tells you about your habits of thought and your view of the world.

Varieties of reading

Consider the range of reading that might be relevant to being a poet. A useful example is Wystan Auden (1906–73). Auden was interested in landscape, geology, Freudian psychology, travel, archaeology and religion (amongst a hundred other things). These passions were strongly individual. They were deep in the composition of his personality. Naturally, the language of this reading, and his subsequent reflections, percolated into his own original poetry.

Any aspiring poet should look at his or her individual reading and interests. The reasons why you are attracted to, for instance, books about the history of mankind or about fast cars, may be a source of both originality and strength in what you write.

What are potential areas of reading for a poet?

- factual texts

- other poetry

- books about poets and poetry

- academic works on literature

- ephemera – magazines, brochures *etc.*

There may be others, but the key point is that a poet who reads only poetry will most likely have a narrow range, be rather academic and introspective. The writer who is immersed in popular culture, who keeps a contemporary attitude, who knows the latest fads and the current idiom of the young, will have a richer source of language.

Gillian Clarke, a Welsh poet, once said in an interview that she set out to write an epic poem about making jam. The interviewer mocked her slightly, assuming that this would be boring and predictable. What he had forgotten was personality, range of interests, humour and so on – the factors that create interest and difference. Reading and conversation provide this unquantifiable depth for a writer.

Poems tell stories

There is also the nature of a poem as a story. In a sense, all poems are short stories. They are a narrative of an experience or a sequence of thinking, however short. As a poet, you should also be a storyteller. The story woven into a poem is a core strength, and there are ways to work on this:

1. Note the plots of the fiction you read.

2. Try to write a prose version, in only 300 words, of the plot.

3. Summarise people, place and events as briefly as possible.

4. Note what adjectives and adverbs add to this.

For instance, you might read a novel, and realise that the storyline could be expressed as:

> Man is unhappy – man meets woman – woman already in a relationship – man still wants her – woman loves him – they leave for a new life.

This could be the basis of a poem about a relationship. But how has the form of the novel, play, short story or television drama expressed that story? How could a poem express the story? This will set you thinking about **form**. Every writer has to choose a form from all the available options, that will suit his or her talents and tastes. To express that plot in a compressed, dense poem, would deal with emotional entanglements of the same kind, but your poetic voice would be the controlling factor.

There are several ways of using your reading. Keep a log, a commonplace book, and monitor statements or images from reading that might contribute to a poem. Often, one line in a text will lead you to a whole new line of thought which grows into a poem. It is common for poets to write sets of poems around a topic or theme, and this might involve wide reading as well as specific research. Keeping a check on the things you read for interest often builds up a useful resource-bank when it comes to the actual writing of a poem.

CASE STUDIES

Alan finds a hidden talent

Alan was in his fifties and had just lost his job. He had worked in public relations most of this life, and had always liked communicating with people. He enjoyed talk, language, reading and planning. He was a sociable person who enjoyed using wit and humour when talking to strangers. Hospitality, welcoming visitors, putting on entertainments, that was his strength.

Now, with time on his hands, the question was, what was he to do with all these redundant abilities and qualities? All he knew was that he wanted to write. He thought that freelance journalism would suit him, as he had contacts in the media world and had networked successfully all his working life. He was still young and active. He had dozens of interests and felt sure that he could write about them.

Alan started writing articles about the work he had done. He submitted one to a magazine about advertising but with no luck. Then several others were sent to various media magazines. The general feedback was that the facts were fine, but too familiar. What editors did like was the imagery, the wit, the one-liners. Alan was at a loss. But by sheer chance, he went to his son's end-of-term concert and there was a guest. The man was a poet who was apparently popular with the teenagers. The stuff he read was funny enough, but hardly what Alan would have called poetry. It didn't rhyme, it was not profound or moving. But he did laugh. It was more like stand-up comedy than poetry.

He thought about that reading for a few days, then as he doodled, at a loss as to what to write next, he realised that the doodles turned into some mini-verses. He wrote several pages of them, all teasing the media people he had worked with – a sort of verbal cartoon sequence.

His son was the one who said, 'Send them of to the editor you know . . . they're a laugh, dad!'

Alan was in demand for fillers at first. Little verses to fill a page. Then it grew by popular demand into a miniature art-form of its own. He always called himself a versifier rather than a poet, but then, that difference may be all snobbery anyway. But he didn't bother with any more articles. One editor pointed out to him that to make the readers laugh was the first step to success. There were too many plain, informative pieces on the editorial desk already.

Jane sees the value of writing honestly

Jane was a student at university. She was involved in producing a student magazine, and her main course was in English literature. She wanted to be a journalist and the magazine production would look impressive on a CV. The editorial team knew that she wrote poetry but that she never wanted to show it to anyone. They wanted a poetry page in the magazine, and asked her to bring her work to show them. She was too shy about it, even though she had owned up to writing poetry once at coffee break. She had actually blushed.

It was only during a tutorial on Wordsworth that her tutor had pointed out that he had once written poetry copying Wordsworth and thrown it all away when he grew older. She asked him why he destroyed it.

'Oh, I never would show it to anyone . . . I wasn't serious about it.'

It was the word 'serious' that set Jane thinking about her own work. The fact was that she had been writing poetry since she was about twelve. She had sat at the kitchen table several nights a week, working on long narrative poems. Of course, she had also written the usual ones – love poems about her favourite singers and actors – all the slushy stuff as she called them. But the truth was that she had a file of about 150 poems of all forms and on a range of subjects. She had never attempted to get one into print.

It was her tutor's comment that made Jane realise why she had been writing. He went on: 'Of course . . . even Emily Brontë didn't really want her work in print . . . *Wuthering Heights* could have been left in a drawer for all she cared. Her sister Charlotte pushed the publishing side of things . . .'

It was settled in her mind. The sequence of poems about her home town and her family were published in the magazine. The plaudits she received soon made her see what writing was all about. Jane's grandma has often told her not to hide her light under a bushel. She had thought it was nonsense – now she understood it was true. Jane started sending poems to magazines and soon made a name for herself. She had worked at the craft, over the years, and been true to her feelings.

DISCUSSION POINTS

1. What would be the benefits of joining a local writing group for someone who wanted to specialise in writing poetry?

2. Is it really possible to write poetry almost 'to order' – like a journalist? If so, isn't that a lower order, maybe verse, not real poetry?

2
Checking on Essential Skills

BUILDING ON YOUR PRESENT SKILLS

Obviously you need certain abilities with words, but it is difficult to lay down rules that would provide some magic formula for poetic success. Dylan Thomas (1914–53) said that he was 'drunk on words' and that the cadences of the language in the Authorised Version of the Bible had a deep influence on him. Some poets have simply written rhymes in the same line-patterns and been content with that. There are certainly no formulae for success. But if you are reading this book, then there must be some *instinct* or *urge* in you to write poetry; that implies a need to write with a sense of play, verbal adventure and a sheer love of the 'sound effects' of language.

There are some indicators as to what latent skills are needed:

● Do you enjoy puns, plays on words?

● Do you respond to satirical rhymes?

● Do you find word-origins interesting?

● Do you read poetry regularly?

● Have you ever written a 'spoof' of a poem?

● Do you revel in original, refreshing language?

Ezra Pound said that literature was news that stayed news (*The ABC of Reading*, Chapter 2). He was hinting here at the whimsical but urgent sense of how a poem handles thought. If you can develop a poem from A to Z and take the reader on an exploration of feeling and thought, rather than tell the reader the result of your thought, then you are inviting someone else to create and respond to fresh, vital language.

Your potential as a poet lies in this pool of the absorbed love of words which lies in you. Poetry condenses and refines thought and feeling down to a minium. It doesn't matter what form or subject you choose, a poet needs certain habits of thought and work, which could perhaps be expressed in this way:

● a constant sensitivity to surroundings

● a love of and fascination with people

● a detached view of the 'subject'

● the ability to monitor one's own reactions

● interest in the questions raised by human life.

In other words, much poetry springs from a fascination with questions about human experience, and about the condition of being alive and living with others. A poet must possess a deep interest in the struggle to express the reality of life and of the enigmas involved in understanding oneself and others.

DECIDING WHAT SUBJECT

Writers will tell you that poetry is the one notable area in which it is virtually impossible to sit and wait for **a subject** to write about. It may be possible to write descriptive verse on almost anything, as was a vogue in the eighteenth century. For example this extract from John Dyer's *Grongar Hill.*

> Below me trees unnumbered rise,
> Beautiful in various dyes,
> The gloomy pine, the poplar blue,
> The yellow beech, the sable yew

This is still poetry of course, but it simply *describes* in verse. A subject will normally *demand* to be written rather than remain under a heap of lumber in your head, waiting for you to find it. Many poets keep notebooks around subject headings, and note all random thoughts, quotes and images to assemble later at their desk, when time and peace are available.

Letting subjects develop naturally

The best poetry grows naturally from personality, disposition and the preoccupations you are absorbed by. W. B. Yeats (1865–1939) once said that from the argument with others we make rhetoric, and from the argument with ourselves we make poetry. He was exaggerating a point that has at heart the notion that the greatest poetry is that which is highly individualised. A poet needs to give both arguments in the same poem, perhaps.

Some very basic questions need to be asked of yourself regarding 'subject'. A process something like this tends to happen in the act of putting a poem together:

> observation/feeling . . .
> notes/images . . .
> comparisons . . .
> sense of structure . . .
> writing of first draft . . .
> second draft *etc.*

It is a complex genesis, but if the urge to express a meaning from your observation or experience is genuine and persistent, then it will happen. You might need several drafts of the poem, but a writer feels instinctively when it is right and should be left as complete.

The subject might be random, but the point is that the form the poem takes will be an integral part of the subject. A poem on one scene can branch out into others. The basic questions to ask yourself are these:

1. What are your abiding, recurrent interests? _____

   _____

2. What areas of life do your reading interests follow? _____

   _____

3. Is most of your thinking about places, people or ideas? _____

   _____

4. Do you tend to 'close off' certain types of thought or feelings in conversation? _____

   _____

These are simply pointers as to what your preoccupations may be, and why. You may be more comfortable writing about ideas than people. This is no problem or weakness, and it's a useful lesson to learn early on.

MONITORING PROGRESS

There are several good reasons for keeping a check on your **progress as a poet**. This monitoring could be done in many different ways:

1. Keeping a logbook of subjects and themes, with drafts.

2. Keeping a record of submissions to writers' groups or editors.

3. Keeping a log of reading of poetry – ideas on form *etc.*

4. Noting the dates of any courses/workshops and who you met/work done.

For most writers, the area of poetry is a difficult one to succeed in quickly. It is an art which demands dedication, originality and patience. The general advice regarding success is that you first need to 'find your voice'. This means that your poems are distinctive. Your 'brand' is on them. The long road to that achievement needs to be recorded and the learning process noted. You may never reach that voice, but learning from models and from professionals will give you every chance.

Practical record-keeping

There are several basic, practical ways of keeping records of your progress as a poet. There are for instance, these on-going methods of work:

●   index-cards for addresses of publications/competitions

●   a notebook for drafts

●   a file for editorial responses and feedback from your peers

●   an alphabetical list of poetic forms with examples

●   a cuttings file for articles, profiles and reviews.

These are all sources for future writing as well as notes on each important step of your own learning. More explanation will help here.

Index cards
To up-date competitions.
To log data on magazines and anthologies.

Editorial feedback
Noting constructive criticism.
Critical service analyses.

Notebook for forms
A 'model' for set, formal poems.
Copying practice to learn technique.

Cuttings file
Highlights statements in reviews to learn form.
Notes modern trends, vogues in publishing.
Checks factual data.

Underlying all this method and meticulous checking on your development, there has to be **self-belief**. Having faith in yourself will sustain you. Even if your work is rejected by editors, do not despair. One of the most influential slim volumes of poetry ever published, A. E. Housman's *A Shropshire Lad* (1896), was printed at the author's expense.

My own files are used all the time, even after 20 years of both writing poetry and writing about poetry and poets. My file contains, for instance, information on regional writers, customs and traditions, rural images, notes on immigrants and much more. All these are involved in the subjects I write about and plan to write more about, when thoughts and information have gathered and been put in my own order. That is the central point: records and logging will reflect *your* order and writing needs.

KEEPING YOUR CREATIVE THINKING ALIVE

Rudyard Kipling said in 1923, 'Words are, of course, the most powerful drug used by mankind.' He was stressing the power of original uses of language. The poetic force of verbal dynamics never fails to impress the reader or listener. Consider some jingles for advertisements such as 'whiter than white', 'naughty but nice' or 'cuddly creatures care'. These all use a common poetic technique of **alliteration** – they use clusters of consonant sounds. This simple method makes them 'stick' in the mind. We love wordplay and jokey language with several layers of meaning.

Concepts and images

This feature of language goes a long way to explaining the creativity noticeable in successful poetry. Often, an **image** or a **pun** will occur naturally and spontaneously in the drafting of a lyric. But it is good practice to 'loosen up' the imagination by cultivating creative thinking. After all, the basic approach of all poetic thinking is comparison. The **metaphor** is the building-block of poetry. It will usually work in this way:

concept A	feature	concept B	feature
poverty	gutter	sky	ambition
smallness	ground	heaven	dreams
routine	earth	stars	aspirations

So Oscar Wilde's wonderful metaphor emerges: 'We are all in the gutter but some of us are looking at the stars' (*Lady Windermere's Fan,* Act III).

A constant search for similarities and comparisons could of course lead to poetry which reads as artificial, too contrived and obscure. The similarities should be powerful and immediate in terms of the meaning conveyed, as in Wilde's image. The habit of mind you need to develop is illustrated by **wordgames** or **graffiti**. It is also often evident in children's natural expression. A child may look up to the sky and shout, 'See a floating camel!' – and the child has seen a cloud in the shape of a camel. The adult was perhaps too embedded in reality, too concerned with mortgages and duties. A poet needs to keep that innocent viewpoint bright and clear.

How can this be done? In your notebook (which should always be in your pocket) jot down any detail of life in the street or workplace or home that catches your eye. Many writers use photographs as spurs to further work or as monitoring of places. You then assemble notes at your desk. The everyday world is packed with symbolic meanings and layers of suggested meanings. For instance, a pawnbroker's sign: three golden balls. The balls suggest play, streetgames; gold suggests value, wealth, mines and so on. But the pawnbroker's itself might be in a slum or in a run-down area. You immediately have a contrast and a potential theme.

Question
Do all poems have to be very original?

Answer
No. The sense of originality and newness that the reader feels may be simply a feel of wit or provocation to thought in one image. The sense of difference will be felt.

Develop the habit of writing lists of mental associations relating to an object or scene that seems interesting to you. In brief, play with words. Not all poetry uses these devices, but rhetorical aspects of language are worth exploring. For instance, note how statements such as 'the past is history' or 'I don't believe in God but I fear Him' carry an invitation to think. The first is from a film trailer. The second is a **paradox** – seeming to contradict itself but having a sub-text about belief. A simple contrast in a metaphor such as 'If my father was the head of our house, my mother was the heart' can be effective.

In other words, poetic language handles the opposite of literal statements, as in:

> *literal* – He was a very old man.
> *metaphorical* (or figurative) – He was as old as the hills.

The second statement is not literally true. It is an image, but a 'dead' one – a **cliché**, and over-used, too-familiar image. Your muscle-flexing to be ready for poetry itself involves the demolition of these clichés. Make the familiar seem new, different.

TAKING YOUR FIRST STEPS

The first steps in any form of writing involve copying. When learning how to paint with watercolours, it seems too ambitious to begin without any knowledge of the techniques of the masters. Yet there are two schools of thought here. The rare genius proves that technique, traditional approach and so on is not absolutely essential knowledge.

But supposing you want to write love poetry. Without a knowledge of how difficult the **sonnet form** is as used by Shakespeare in his sequence of 154 sonnets, all about love in some way, your love poetry may be the poorer.

Writing short forms of poetry

One can never be sure, but simply to attempt a style or form from a classic poet can only be beneficial. There are hundreds to choose from, but a useful beginning is to try to write short forms. The **rhyming couplet**, the **epigram** and the **haiku** are all interesting poetic forms to try, simply to test the ground.

Rhyming couplet

In the hands of the masters, such as the eighteenth-century satirist Alexander Pope, this can be powerful. It generally has eight or ten syllables, each line using end-rhyme:

> While pensive poets painful vigil keep,
> Sleepless themselves to give their readers sleep.

These are two lines from a long poem entirely in couplets, written to attack the mediocre talents Pope saw around him. Note the ten syllables in each line, and note also that the second syllables are the stressed ones.

Epigram

This is simply a couplet isolated to make a strong point. Here is Pope again:

> In the lines that you sent are the muses and graces,
> You have the nine in your wit and three in your faces.
> > (*Epigrams I*)

or, more neatly, again Pope, writing an epigraph:

> I am his Highness' dog at Kew.
> Pray tell me sir, whose dog are you?
> > (On the collar of a dog given to Frederick, Prince of Wales)

Haiku

This is a popular form for learning the art of metre – the use of stressed and unstressed syllables in particular patterns and lengths of line. It is a Japanese form in origin, having only three lines, with a pattern of 5, 7, 5 syllables.

> In the old man's face 5
> Deep lines are an athlete's tracks 7
> He has run his race 5

Normally, a haiku simply describes nature, as in:

> Under green cover 5
> Spring is breaking unnoticed 7
> Winter's game over 5

These are rhymed in lines one and three, but rhyme is not essential. Whatever you copy simply as an exercise, it will start you reflecting on the idea of form and the usefulness of a particular technique for your subject. But there are other ways.

Prose to verse
You can start by simply writing a prose summary of the subject. Suppose you have a poem in mind on a scene in a country village in spring. The prose might begin:

Silence all around. It recalls an exam room. But it's a warm, clear evening. A cat and a blackbird disturb the peace. There's a hunt in progress. Stalking.

Work on each separate piece of meaning and give it a line:

> Silence – like an exam room.
> There's a hush in the warm evening air,
> a cat treading the stones.
> The blackbird sings goodbye to the day.

Finally, add some heightening, some dramatic detail:

> Silence like an examination room;
> a hush in this bright warm evening.
> Only the cat's tread on stone
> and the blackbird's elegy to day.

This illustrates well how the sheer 'spadework' required in writing a poem is so steady but worthwhile. You need patience and a sense of editing.

CASE STUDIES

John finds inspiration

John was determined to find something to write about on his day on the moors. He had just joined a local writers' group and a competition had been set for the best piece of poetry on a desolate place. He was fond of walking in the Lake District, so he set off early, and by mid-day he was on the fells, camera over his shoulder and notebook ready.

He stopped regularly to note the hovering birds, the changing colours of the sky, the lichen on the rocks. People kept passing him, smiling and saying hello. The day went on. He took dozens of photographs for inspiration when he sat down at his desk, in need of reminders of what had been seen.

By dusk, he was tired but really had no idea how to 'use' all this data. It was the same when he sat down with sheaves of random notes and a plethora of photographic images to choose from. There was really nothing special about a description of nature. It has all been said before, for example by Wordsworth and more recently, by Ted Hughes and Seamus Heaney.

John had missed the real potential in the day's experience: the people. All the walkers had words, stories and experiences. It was all there to be 'tapped into' if he had made the time to chat. This only occurred to him at the writers' group, when he read his best effort but confessed that it was quite ordinary, then realised that most other writers had included dialogue, descriptions of faces and so on. It was all a matter of the ordinary in an extraordinary setting.

Sally finds a workable method

Sally's problem was how to actually write drafts of poems. By this she meant the practical difficulty of using notepaper, space, word-processor or anything that would help. Her normal practice was to scribble on loose sheets of paper and then clip them together, discarding the poor material when she was satisfied. But this was chaotic. Sheets were sometimes lost. Once she spilled coffee on one draft.

She tried using a word-processor but somehow she felt she needed to *see* every correction, all the potentially usable lines and so on. A creative writing programme on television gave her the answer. In an interview, a well-known poet described how he used a thick A4 notebook, then used a whole page for one section or stanza, while on the opposite page only the acceptable lines were written. He also wrote only with a pencil, a sharp HB, hard and suitable for fine writing. He could erase words and lines when certain that they could not be used.

As with so many things, the solution to Sally's problem was very simple. It just needed some practical advice from someone with experience. It was part of a schools programme that she watched because she combed the television magazines every week, noting anything of interest to writers.

It is now common practice and Sally could not go about writing poems in any other way. The point is, it worked *for her.*

DISCUSSION POINTS

1. What are the main considerations for a writer who wants to specialise in poetry when joining a local writers' circle?

2. What data should be included in notebooks when monitoring submissions to magazines?

3
Working on Skills – I

UNDERSTANDING FORMAL POETRY

Poetry in a specific form has been the traditional conception of poetry in our society for centuries. The idea that poetry can take any form and be written almost whimsically is relatively recent. Of course, poetry generally is spontaneous, but that is a different issue. Form means that the rhythm, the lines, the rhyme and the overall shape and structure of the poem follow certain rules. As noted in Chapter 1, the rules stem from classical literature and relate to the Greek and Latin writers who have been widely studied and imitated in our culture.

Features of formal poetry
Formal poetry generally has these features:

- patterns of rhymed words at the end of lines

- a repeated rhythm created by metrical elements

- a set length (number of lines)

- groups of lines or rhymes used in contrast.

The questions arise as to why this is the case, and do poets still write formal poetry? Indeed they do, and the reason is related to (a) the technical challenge of the art form and (b) certain forms are admirable for most poetic subjects. This is easily illustrated by a stanza from Tennyson's *In Memoriam*, written in 1850 after the death of his friend, Arthur Hallam:

> Dark house, by which once more I stand,
> Here in the long, unlovely street,
> Doors where my heart was used to beat
> So quickly, waiting for a hand.

Notice that each line has **eight stressed syllables**. Traditional poems are written in terms of **metrical feet** and two syllables make one metrical foot. So this stanza has 'four foot' lines or **tetrameter**. The commonest forms in English poetry have these line-lengths:

trimeter – 3
tetrameter – 4
pentameter – 5
hexameter – 6

Hexameters are not so often met, and there are instances of very short lines of only two feet (**dimeter**) as in some ballads and songs, but the majority of poems are in 3, 4 or 5 foot lines.

Rhyme-schemes
Tennyson's stanza rhymes in the pattern of **ABBA**, as the custom is to label the first end-rhyme A and so on through the alphabet:

stand – A
street – B
beat – B
hand – A

It is clearly a poem with profound emotion beneath it. The repeated lines and rhymes develop the emotive power so that most stress is placed on 'hand' at the end, referring to the dead friend.

There are many forms in traditional poetry of this kind, and there will be further examples in this chapter. Even a poor attempt at writing such a demanding form will teach you valuable skills and give you a unique insight into some of the craft involved.

WRITING FREE VERSE

In contrast to formal poetry is the concept of **free verse**. This term implies that anything goes: that form is unimportant. In fact, this variety can be just as difficult to write. Free verse, as written notably by Walt Whitman, the American poet, in his *Leaves of Grass* (1855) might look chaotic on the page, but it has a **rhythm** and a **structure**. It reflects a spontaneous, inner sense of rhythm following the cadences of speech and of thinking. Here is an example of free verse:

My friend sits silently behind newspapers,
talking to his woman.
He hides in a symphony, alone in its flood,
talking to his woman.
When he is with me we spend endless hours,
him talking about her
but saying nothing.

Note how three main features work here:

1. The 'white space' forcing a pause as you read.

2. The statements are short, building up to the last line.

3. Long and short lines are used.

The staggered, short statements gradually develop to the final contradiction. Another feature is the way that free verse allows sharp,
isolated imagery as in the 'symphony' image. The reader takes more
notice of such an image, than a string of images in a structured,
narrative poem.

A modern idiom

Free verse is suitable to the **modern idiom**, in which we expect powerful or double-edged incisive statements about contemporary issues.
The influence of the mass media is clearly observed in this. Such
poems can be very fulfilling to write successfully, but the only way
to work is to follow your instincts regarding your 'inner voice' as you
write. There are, however, some general guidelines:

● avoid too many repeated similar lines

● use verbs or subjects clearly

● keep to the grammar and syntax over long statements

● guide the reader through changes of mood directly

● rewrite, cutting out words which have no function.

EXPLORING THE CRAFT: THE SONNET

Of all the established poetic forms, the **sonnet** is the one most suited to an explanation of what has been said so far about the advantages of writing to a pattern. It may seem like a literary 'straightjacket' to be disciplined in these ways, but an aspiring writer needs to dip into a range of techniques and forms to find a personal voice.

Five main types of poetry

The overall body of poetry in English breaks into these broad types:

> lyric
> narrative
> dramatic
> descriptive
> humorous.

In the **lyric** category, the main forms are **elegy, ode, song, sonnet**, and **religious forms** such as **hymns**. Lyric poetry in classical Greece was originally recited to the accompaniment of a lyre, a stringed instrument. The origins of the sonnet are similarly in song. The name means literally a 'sound piece', coming originally from Italian literature.

Three forms of sonnet

In English, there are three main forms:

Shakespearian – rhyme scheme:	ABABCDCDEFEFGG
Regular/Italian – rhyme scheme:	ABBAABBACDECDE
Miltonic – rhyme scheme:	as Italian, but with CDCDCD in the last lines

Keeping to the Shakespearian version, these are the names of the sections of the standard 14 lines:

ABABCDCDEFEF	=	3 quatrains (a group of four lines)
GG	=	final rhyming couplet (2 lines)

This is a classic example from Shakespeare:

Shall I compare thee to a summer's day?
Thou art more lovely and more temperate.
Rough winds do shake the darling buds of May,
And summer's lease hath all too short a date.
Sometime too hot the eye of heaven shines,
And often is his gold complexion dimmed;
And every fair from fair sometime declines,
By chance, or nature's changing course, untrimmed;
But thy eternal summer shall not fade,
Nor lose possession of that fair thou ow'st,
Nor shall Death brag thou wanderest in his shade,
When in eternal lines to time thou grow'st.
So long as men can breathe or eyes can see,
So long lives this, and this gives life to thee.

(Sonnet 18)

Note how the basic thinking is simple:

(1) beauty fades like the seasons
(2) you are beautiful
(3) but your beauty will be immortal
(4) why? because of this lyric, which will be read in years to come,
    after your death.

This disciplined development of a clear line of thought is a total learning experience for anyone serious about being a poet. There is a craftsmanship to be learnt, despite Hugh McDiarmid's quip that 'Our principal writers have all been fortunate in escaping a regular education.'

Practical sonnet-writing

How do you go about writing a sonnet? The next section develops this by looking at metre, but note that this process is still useful:

1. Write a prose version of your reasoning in 300 words.

2. Work on the **quatrain**, finding rhymes by trial and error.

3. Have a **thesaurus** on your desk – or a **rhyming dictionary**.

4. Try the final couplet when you can write your final 'clinching' statement in one sentence.

CONSTRUCTING METRICAL FORMS

The study of 'beats per line' is properly known as **prosody** or **metrics**. The **metre** idea stems from Greek poetry and is based on the metrical feet as explained earlier. In English poetry, the patterns of stress making them **feet** are most commonly these:

● **iambic** – second syllable stress -/

● **trochaic** – first syllable stressed /-

● **anapaestic** – stress – stress – unstress //-

● **dactylic** – stress – unstress – unstress /- -

Notice the **iambic** and **trochaic** are 2 syllable feet and that **dactylic** and **anapaestic** are 3 syllable feet. It is easier to remember ordinary words for each type:

iambic – occur

trochaic – weekly

anapaestic – serenade

dactyllic – credulous

When beginning to write in metrical forms, it is best to keep to iambic as in the classic Shakespearean line known as blank verse. This is **iambic pentameter**:

> Now is the winter of our discontent
> (*Richard III*, I:1)

note the five feet, each foot iambic. This gives the 'feel' of the great dramatic speeches from Shakespeare, but blank verse is also associated with much eighteenth century, Romantic and Victorian poetry.

Metre for humour

The **anapaest** and **dactyl** obviously suit humorous verse forms, as in limericks:

> There was a young lady from Leeds
> Who swallowed a packet of seeds.
> When they began to take root,
> She made lots of loot
> Meeting all your garden needs.

The first line is **dactylic** and the last is **anapaestic**. It doesn't matter, in terms of **prosody** in contemporary poetry, what mixtures of lines you produce. The only rule is that it *reads well* and meets your *intended purpose*. The secret is always to read aloud. That pinpoints the fluency and the strength; it also highlights where the weaknesses and errors are.

There are dozens of metrical forms. The main ones are included in the glossary of this book, and you can only benefit from trying metrical forms if you persevere. You really have to want to concentrate on this type of poetry to overcome the hard apprenticeship.

USING THE RIGHT DICTION

Form, prosody and **rhyme schemes** are only a part of the craft of poetry, however. The fundamental components are the words: the basis of the entire art. Traditionally, until the period of Modernism in the early twentieth century, there was a well-defined category of language (*diction* being the usual literary term) for poetry. It was related to standard English but also to a literary tradition of so-called **poetic diction**. We are able to observe this diction in the central body of English poetry written through the centuries. However, it bore little relation to the English actually spoken:

> Stern eagle of the far north-west,
> Thou that bearest in thy grasp the thunderbolt
> (Sir Walter Scott)

or:

> No voice divine the storm alloyed,
> No light propitious shone
> (William Cowper)

Since Wordsworth tried to introduce 'the language of common men' into poetry at the end of the eighteenth century, there has been more awareness of the range of diction available to poets, from dialect to jargon or even media-based mid-Atlantic. Today anything goes regarding diction. Our society is now multicultural, and the sheer vitality and adaptability of 'world English' makes it ideal for the sinews and flesh of meanings put on the skeleton of structure we have looked at.

Question
Is it possible to write poetry 'just as you speak' or is that frowned upon?

Answer
Yes, it is possible, although possibilities are limited, and variety is always crucial if you don't want to bore your readers.

Choose your idiom

You can choose your **idiom**. Decide at an early stage how you want to express ideas and in what available contemporary idiom. There is a vast spectrum, from proper and formal to slang and dialect. A simple way to grasp the importance of this is to play around with supplying a missing word from a line. These lines from a poem on the death of a grandfather have a blank space. Supply a suitable word.

> He never . . . . why dying was so hard;
> he just told us what he saw
> in the patterns of the wallpaper.

The missing word is 'asked' but equally it could be 'questioned' or 'moaned' and so on. One word would change everything else. No matter what else you attend to, always select the active words with care and try different **synonyms** in the syntax of the poem. Have a thesaurus handy.

Poetry revitalises

The important guidelines on diction all relate to the idea that poetry is the one version of a language which constantly seeks to **revitalise** words and the way we understand each other – the way we experience life. Poetry prevents the moribund, played-out words from making thought and feeling stale. Consider a simple example of this range of options from a thesaurus.

> *refuse*: say no, shake one's head, deny, declaim, decline, turn down, spurn . . .

This list shows perfectly how fine nuances of meaning totally change impact, overall sense and emotional force. The colloquial, chatty 'shake one's head' compared with 'decline' is totally different in application.

An interesting point here is that, in the days when standard English ruled, there was really only one audience for poetry. But now we have dozens of 'audiences' each with a sense of what 'diction' they want to hear in the discourse of their poetry. There are several constructive steps you can take here:

●   Collect local or occupational slang.

●   Note and adapt the metaphors of colloquial, everyday talk.

●   Change the word order or replace 'tired' words with new.

●   Write mixtures of standard and regional diction.

●   Note, copy and use the speech idiom you need.

Look at the notebooks of writers (for instance Raymond Chandler) to learn how notes about language have been transmuted into poetry.

CASE STUDIES

Peter's education has to be overcome!

Peter's experience of poetry had been confined to the classics. His taste reflected that of his masters at school and Milton, Tennyson, Rupert Brooke were deemed acceptable. Poetry was clearly meant to be written in the special 'coded' language of these writers – all university men. There was poetry and there was rubbish – 'verse' – such as you find on birthday cards.

This was no problem until Peter felt the urge to write something creative himself. He tried stories at first, but then heard a 'performance poet' on television and was, against his better judgement, impressed. Poetry had actually made him laugh and think, and it had been about something other than trees, flowers and mountains.

When he tried to write, however, all that came into his head were images stemming from 'I wandered lonely as a cloud' poems or simply banal clichés. Peter joined a class at the local college of further education; it was a revelation. They spent three weeks doing nothing but reading modern poetry and copying ideas. 'Just to unlearn things', the lecturer said.

It was week six when the first triumph arrived. A 'list poem' was set, like the sort of thing Julie Andrews had sung about in 'These are a few of my favourite things'. Peter just listed his loves in life at random, and to his surprise, the class liked it all.

Peter did not destroy his volumes of Wordsworth and Milton, but he spent an increasing amount of time at the library finding out what contemporary poets wrote about. He was set free to write without 'influences' and so found his own taste and his own angle on life.

Jill stops reading the metre

Jill had been writing poetry for several years. She had been published in an assortment of magazines, having found her forte as a 'versifier', supplying neat comic verses and epigrams. Editors knew what to expect from her and her poems were good 'fillers' if they had half a page to fill.

But she became bored. Jill was a member of various writing groups and journals, newsletters and publications regularly dropped through the letterbox. They were full of 'serious' poetry, often in free forms, without any of the rhythm and metre she had always worked at.

Jill had plenty of ideas, but they were all humorous ones. The philosophical, introverted writing in most of the small magazines was foreign to her. She tried to read up on the poets who had succeeded at this. Her objective was to be taken seriously and be published alongside some of these regulars who were quite obviously well thought of by critics and editors.

The break came with Jill's chance reading of an old handbook on literature. It suggested writing with a number of stresses in the lines but in random places. The book pointed out that simple description of what is before you is the way forward. Jill worked at that, turning prose into short lines with three of four stresses in each line. She began to be read – and taken seriously.

DISCUSSION POINTS

1. How could you find out about poetry in local dialects – and what markets exist for such writing?

2. If you wanted to concentrate on writing formal, metrical poetry, would that mean it would be harder to get into print? Suggest some reasons and possibilities.

4
Working on Skills – II

THINKING ABOUT IMAGERY

A simple definition of imagery is a type of language-use which expresses similarities and comparisons, rather than giving direct, literal truth. When Lord Byron writes:

> Now, where the swift Rhone cleaves his way between
> heights, which appear as lovers who have parted
> in hate . . .

he is using the clearest type of imagery. He just compares two hills to two estranged lovers.

If you can use imagery well, then you have given your poetry its true 'bite' – its immediate effect. Readers will recognise a visual image more quickly and clearly than a deep thought or intellectual argument. The principal guidelines in using imagery can be expressed in these questions:

● Is this thought or feeling best written as an image?

● Does the image have a freshness, a vitality?

● Is the comparison too long and complex?

● Does the image read as a natural part of the poem – not forced or affected?

Four common types of image
There are various types of images, but the commonest are these:

simile	**personification**
metaphor	**symbol.**

Similes

A **simile** (pronounced sim-i-li) is a direct comparison of two things, using the words 'as' or 'like'. In ordinary speech we may say, 'as white as snow' or 'As quick as a greyhound'. In a poem, there has to be some appeal, some easily-perceived freshness:

> Like as the waves make towards the pebbled shore,
> So do our minutes hasten to their end.

Metaphors

A **metaphor** is also a comparison but with more detail and subtlety and which is prolonged more than a simile:

> A little learning is a dangerous thing;
> Drink deep, or taste not the Pierian spring:
> There shallow draughts intoxicate the brain,
> And drinking largely sobers us again.
>   (Alexander Pope, *An Essay on Criticism*)

(NB the Pierian Spring is the fabled fountain of poetic inspiration.)

Personification

Personification is a method of making inanimate things take on human or animal qualities. Gerard Manley Hopkins wrote to express despair in his poem, *The Wreck of the Deutschland*, which tells the story of loss of life at sea:

> Hope had grown grey hairs.
> Hope had mourning on.

Rather than say, literally, 'There was no hope', Hopkins personifies 'Hope' as a 'person', an entity who is dying.

Symbols

A **symbol** (see next section) is a direct placing of an image or word that represents something, such as 'the red rose of England' or 'the white dove of peace'. In Shakespeare's play *Macbeth* the tragic hero knows that his end is near; Shakespeare gives him these words:

My way of life is fallen into the sere,
the yellow leaf.

(Macbeth, V:3)

The yellow leaf symbolises Macbeth's decay. It is the quickest, most vivid image. To use symbols intelligently and in the best place is one of the most powerful uses of imagery in poetry.

APPLYING SYMBOLS

How can you practise the use of symbols? There are several exercises which may prove useful here.

1. 'Editing' to a symbol

Stage one
Write a full description: The fish were all dead in the pool. Their silver bellies were turned up to the light. Not one of them had survived.

Stage two
Shorten this to one statement. The silver bellies of the dead fish glinted in the light.

Stage three
Introduce a symbolic way of saying this: Death shone in the silver bellies. You could carry on editing until you were happy with what you have.

2. Lists

Stage one
Write a descriptive list: Winter. Grey clouds. Oppressive. Dirty streets. A dead cat by the road, tarmac smeared with blood.

Stage two
Keep the most meaningful image: the dead cat?
The season of the dead cat by the road.
Winter. Grey jaws, hungry for life.

3. Short forms – using one symbol
For example, the **haiku**.

Summer wore red gowns:
Showed the starry bracelets well.
Who thinks of the dead?

This combines personification (Summer) with a symbol – 'Starry bracelets' = the stars of a summer sky.

Symbols are the very basic materials of poetic expression. Our minds love to work in visual or sensual ways, and poems that really succeed will appeal to that need in the reader's imagination. Even a simple progression from (a) literal statement to (b) one single image often produces a symbol quite naturally, without being forced.

LEARNING HOW TO DESCRIBE

Description is one of the bases of all writing, in a sense. Consider a typical entry in a writer's notebook. You have been in a city centre at the height of summer. What you might have seen, as the basis of a potential lyric poem, is a foreign visitor trying to buy something at a market stall:

> Sweltering sun. In the open market, a constant hubbub. Lots of tourists. Party of French visitors at a souvenir stall. Stall has London bobbies, miniatures of Big Ben *etc*. Busker singing. Homeless people silent, mugs on their knees, waiting for coins to chinkle in the pot. Young Frenchman tries to buy a tee-shirt. All talk is in the gestures, pointing, holding . . . eventually the seller and the buyer laugh.

There is a great deal of poetic potential here, simply because there is detail. Notice how the observation has taken in three elements.

● the atmosphere (mood)

● the contrasts in British society (social comment)

● people (a conflict, contrast, communication).

Description involves being aware of how we perceive and understand the world through language. Consider three ways of saying the same thing:

1. The light reflected from the water on the road.

2. The water shone like varnish on the road.

3.   The road seemed like an endless sheet of water.

Each one puts the stress on a slightly different 'way of seeing' what's in the writer's mind. The image of a 'varnish' helps to make the sight more immediately comprehensible.

Improve your descriptive skills
There are several ways of doing this:

● Use words that are simple but exact.

● Mix 'concrete' words with abstract.

● Mix specific detail with general facts.

● Write images only when particularly effective.

'Concrete' refers to the things we can see, touch, be aware of in the real physical world. Abstract is the opposite – intangible ideas and concepts.

Example
For example, the line:

> The walls flaked and splintered.

uses concrete language. You can 'see' the wall and how far it is disintegrating. But this is a line using abstract words:

> Art never expresses anything but itself.
> (Oscar Wilde, *The Decay of Lying*)

It is also helpful to appreciate the many ingredients which have helped create the English language. Germanic, French and Latin vocabulary are all mixed in our current dictionary, in addition to American and Commonwealth influences. But consider these different words for the same thing:

operative – worker
amicable – friendly
cordial – warm

The first column has Latin/French origin (called Romance languages) whereas the second column stem from Saxon (Germanic) earlier versions of English. The Latin-based words will generally tend to be more difficult for your reader to grasp than the Germanic-based ones. Imagine for example the difference between using **domicile** as opposed to **home**.

Dialects and realism
Some poets have consciously used a poetic diction which is predominantly 'Anglo-Saxon' in nature:

> And there for me the apple tree
> Do lean down low on Linden Lea.
> (William Barnes *My Orchard in Linden Lea*)

In most English dialect poetry, you can soon be aware of this feature. As a rough guideline, it is probably better to use a Saxon word instead of a Latinate one when you are describing something concrete. Realism is most easily achieved with this in mind.

Of course, you may want to write intellectual poetry, dealing in ideas rather than in everyday experience of life. Many successful modern poets have done this, but if you do, you may narrow your range of readership, even if your status and esteem with the critics will rise.

WRITING BY COPYING FORMS

All the skills discussed so far can be worked at steadily. As discussed earlier, there is nothing wrong with copying some set form of poetry in order to learn. Take a rather loosely defined form which is well-known – the **elegy**. This is generally defined as a poem which laments, often a death or a loss. In fact, the term is used of any solemn, reflective poem such as the famous *Elegy written in a Country Churchyard* by Thomas Gray (1751). This poem provides a classic example of the benefits of learning by copying.

The section on metre above explained **iambic pentameter** or **blank verse**. Gray's poem is in this metre, so you have a chance to learn about blank verse by writing a stanza (any verse or section). Gray's opening line shows this:

> The curfew tolls the knell of parting day

Read this aloud and over-stress the line. You will 'hear' the blank verse, or the iambic foot (unstress–stress). Now, simply take some notes or a photograph of a scene you wish to describe, and copy the rhythm as you draft. You might have these notes:

Midnight. Summer. Party music in town. Thump of the disco beat. Wrappers in the street. Strong breeze.

Work on the line by writing one statement:

The throbs and disco sounds defeat the wind.

This line is in blank verse. I had to work at this, cancelling out words from my first draft, but I eventually had the right metre.

All this has the same attraction as a crossword or a wordgame, but its value lies in your gradual awareness of a sense of poetic rhythm. Your own 'inner voice' will start to emerge quite naturally as you feel the sense of the melody in a statement.

This copying process can be summarised like this:

●   Find a form that deals with your subject area.

●   Read widely in anthologies.

●   Choose and note the metre/form of a poem.

●   Copy by drafting from prose to verse.

●   Count the syllables (beats) as you work.

●   Edit by changing words to match the metrical line.

Question
Does copying forms and metre inhibit my creativity?

Answer
Not at all. It simply provides confidence in a craft, boosted by use of skills. The innate creativity will always come through if your feeling and response to experience is always genuine.

USING REGIONAL LANGUAGE

In the nineteenth century it became fashionable to write in local dialect, particularly as the fast-developing northern industrial towns cultivated civic and regional pride. The verse was mostly comic and sentimental, usually narrative or dealing with love and death. In Yorkshire West Riding mill towns, local poetry was widely read and published in 'almanacs' for the working class who, particularly after the 1870 Education Act, provided a growing market for enterprising publishers of local writing.

The tradition lives on, notably on a regional scale. There are dialect societies which encourage such poetry by producing newsletters and anthologies. But obviously, if you choose to write in a local dialect, you are restricting your readership to one defined group.

Why do people write in dialect?

● nostalgia for a fading community life

● a sense of history and belonging

● a love of the humour in dialect expression

● political, radical and class reasons.

The standard literary English discussed above clearly gives us a reason why dialect poetry thrived a century ago. There was a sense of 'them and us' and 'North and South' and many poets disapproved of the status and power of the London literary establishment which had no time for regional writing.

The appeal of dialect poetry can be understood easily by reading Robert Burns, the first successful dialect poet in English/Scottish literature. The familiar lines from his poem on a mouse illustrate this:

> Wee sleekit, cowerin', tim'rous beastie,
> O what a panic's in thy breastie.
> Thou need na start awa sae hasty,
> Wi' bickering brattle!

This is fairly readable, for someone with no knowledge of Scots dialect, and a reader can guess or 'feel' the meaning of words such as 'sleekit' or 'brattle' without recourse to a dictionary, and the poem makes us feel and react to a common experience.

Seeing dialect verse into print

Writing in dialect can achieve startling effects. If you want to use your knowledge of a local dialect or slang, then why not? It can be fun writing mixtures of standard English and dialect, but more than that – it can also be an innovative approach to handling familiar subjects in a more daring and challenging way.

The best start in this variety of poetry is to find information on dialect societies (see the Useful Addresses section) and also check out local and county magazines for potential markets.

CASE STUDIES

Joan uses her imagination

The writing circle had set a general task for all members. One week to write a poem on the idea of 'My Memory Box'. The exercise was to imagine ten items from your life that you would treasure in this imaginery box.

Joan tried several approaches, all based on different forms, from sonnet to elegy, then in rhyming couplets. None of her efforts seemed 'natural' or related to her own life in any way. She phoned a friend in the circle – a prolific writer who advised her to: 'Just write the list first, then use natural language that comes out of the old human computer.'

She did. The approach worked well. It was in free verse, of course. This was something she found difficult as she had been reared in classic, formal verse at school. But the ease with which free verse linked with the spontaneous writing of prose descriptions helped her enormously.

Joan wrote poetry far more regularly, and made a point of reading the best contemporary poetry.

Henry writes his own lingo

It was Henry's friend, Robert who suggested it. 'Harry – you're naturally funny – your stories I mean.' Every tea-break at work, Henry had a story to tell to a captive audience. The tales were developed from real experiences. The secret of their success was that he told them with his natural accent, peppering the tales with dialect words such as 'gawp' for 'stare' and 'laik' for 'play'. He was a Yorkshireman, and the words were innately funny.

Other friends gave such a good response that one day at lunchtime, he wrote some rhymes about the people in his stories. He is now a prominent member of a dialect society. They have regular meetings and they publish a newsletter about Yorkshire dialect. The writers in the group are in demand for local functions and radio, as members are always happy to recite and perform.

Henry is the local bard. 'If we lived in Wales, they'd crown you as a druid!' his friends said. The stories kept coming, and Henry is called on for local radio and television if there is a local item needing some distinct Tyke character.

DISCUSSION POINTS

1. 'The best description gives us smells, sense of touch. We feel the scene.' What types of poetic language can achieve this?

2. What sort of subject suits a short poem such as a haiku or an epigram? Is there one, or can any subject be written about in a short form?

5
Applying Rhyme and Reason

PRACTISING WITH RHYME

A common misconception about poetry is that rhyme is always of one kind and for one purpose. It's easy to assume that rhyme is there simply to complete a thought, give a contrast or suggest finality. In other words, it is used obviously or repetitively. For instance, this simple stanza from the folk song 'The Wild Rover' illustrates a common use of rhyme:

> I've been a wild rover
> for many a year,
> I've spent all my money
> on whisky and beer.

The listener or reader anticipates the end rhyme as soon as the last word of the first line is read or spoken. The 'ear' expects the rhyme.

Naturally, this is common in a great amount of poetry, but there are far more subtle and innovative ways of using rhyme to communicate a whole gamut of thoughts, moods and emotions. First, notice that rhyme can be used in ways other than simple end-rhyme:

> The days were fine when you were mine.

is an internal rhyme. It is given inside the line with the fine/mine coupling (sometimes called a **medial rhyme**). Some rhymes may be imperfect, 'eye' rhymes such as move/love when they 'rhyme' only on sight, not when spoken.

Some useful devices

Far more interesting and vibrant are these devices:

Assonance – closeness of vowel sounds, mostly in stressed syllables.

Consonance – closeness and matching of consonant sounds.
Feminine rhyme – rhymes with two syllables, stressed on the
                    first.

Examples

Assonance: 'The mind gone, moaning lone'
Consonance: 'Too weak to strike,
                    to hit out at might and work
                    – from a corner lurk.'
Feminine rhyme: 'There were the sober Roman column
                    where the armies stand, still and solemn.'

These are all the main 'nuts and bolts' of obvious, purposeful
rhyme. What about the subtle, highly original poetry which uses
rhyming technique? The first stanza of John Donne's 'The Sun
Rising' does much that you can learn from:

> Busy old fool, unruly sun,
> Why dost thou thus,
> Through windows, and through curtains call on us?
> Must to thy motions lovers' seasons run?
> Saucy pedantic wretch, go chide
> Late schoolboys, and sour prentices,
> Go tell court-huntsmen, that the king will ride,
> Call country ants to harvest offices;
> Love, alike, no seasons knows, nor clime,
> Nor hours, days, months, which are the rags of time.

This lyric has all the stylistic devices about writing rhyme that you
need to know and practise. These are:

● using run-on (enjambment)

● having caesuras (pauses) in the middle of lines

● breaking up the 'tempo' with punctuation

● writing 'lists' to give emphasis.

Run on or enjambment: this is where a line is not punctuated at the
end, so the reader reads on without a breath-pause to stress the feeling ('go chide/late . . .).

Caesura: a meaningful pause within a line, for effect ('through windows, and through curtains').

Punctuation: note the four commas in the penultimate line, all 'slowing' the reading speed.

Lists: in the final line, the list of short words gives extra emphasis to the last image 'the rags of time' which is the completion of the final couplet.

This may seem technical and difficult, but you should start with couplets and four-line stanzas, using all the types of rhyme. It is the most flexible and serviceable stylistic ploy – usable in comic and in serious poetry. So what are the practical guidelines?

● Start with short forms (ballads, couplets).

● Write comedy and satire first.

● Try assonance for a descriptive piece.

The next section looks in detail at one 'practice' piece.

KNOWING WHEN AND HOW TO RHYME

A basic question is about the contexts in which rhyme is a definite strength and those in which free verse is to be preferred. There is no simple answer, but generally, these patterns can be observed:

● End-rhyme is perfect for comedy and satire.

● All rhymes, thoughtfully used, are suitable for love and religious poetry.

● Free verse is predominantly for serious subjects.

● There are no absolute rules, despite these trends.

The best way to learn is to develop a short lyric, using two developments into poems.

1. The basic idea.
   note: shop-window full of second-hand goods. Many bought as expensive gifts and not used? Looks like a sandy sea-bed.

2. When you have the basic similarity, write lists of ways to describe undersea objects.

3. Then write descriptively but simply, using the image:
   'Here they lie in heaps, cast-offs,
   barnacled with dirt,
   piled like sunken pottery on the sea-bed.'

4. To rhyme or not to rhyme?

In this poem, the image carried enough strength of meaning to complete a short poem. But a rhyme will often emerge early in your thinking, and one good, effective couplet will demand to be developed into a rhymed poem.

The question of how to rhyme involves three general considerations;

● Would rhyme add anything important?

● Is the poem convincing without rhyme?

● Has the effort to rhyme somehow been 'forced'?

Question
How does one know if a rhymed or unrhymed version is best?

Answer
There is no certain way of knowing until two versions are written, but if a poem is generally better in free verse, why not use a final rhyming couplet for effect? It would work this way, but not vice versa.

CHOOSING COMIC FORMS

Contrary to the general opinion, writing comic poetry is not just a matter of limericks and Stanley Holloway monologues. What is crucial here, though, is rhyme. Think of humour in verse and you think of a clever rhyme. Most poems of this type use a limited range of techniques. The important English speciality is surreal nonsense as in Edward Lear, Thomas Hood and Lewis Carroll. Forms are usually short, ironic and direct. Here are some examples of the types:

Understatement

Epitaph for the last tram in Leeds.

> Rattling red monster astride the lines,
> running through my youth
> with other joys like Woodbines,
> noisy, gauche, alien, uncouth,
> you emerged from yellow city fog
> cracking in like fate.
> Shame about Mrs Mason's dog,
> who crossed the road quite late.

The last two lines carry the humour, the penultimate line seeming to change the tone and the last line being flat and ordinary.

Bathos

'From the sublime to the ridiculous' – this is the first stanza of a poem on 'My Old Schoolmaster':

> To the heavenly thud of willow on leather,
> we listened hard to J G F Pennyfeather.
> He taught us history, but what is greater,
> he taught us all to honour pater.

Again, the last two lines have the effect. There is a 'change of gear' down to the banality of the last line.

Satire

The English speciality of abuse and ridicule is the most manageable type of comic poem. For this, you need a target. For Alexander Pope it was often the folly of the very wealthy.

> What Nature wants, commodious Gold bestows,
> 'Tis thus we eat the bread another sows;
> But how unequal it bestows, observe,
> Tis thus we riot while who sow it, starve.
>
> *(Epistle to Arbuthnot)*

You have to note what all these examples have in common: a zest in the force of the wry, ironic vision of people or a sense of the absurd in life. It can be worked at steadily, and couplets are a good way to begin. The first consideration should always be to communicate your sense of absurdity, rage or nonsense.

LEARNING FROM MODELS BY THE BEST

This is an example of a modern comic form, and it is a useful one to work on and develop:

> E. C. Bentley
> Quite accidentally
> Invented this verse form of wit,
> And this is it.
>
> (anon)

This is the clerihew, after Bentley's middle name. The idea is to comment on a famous person and make a satirical remark. The first two lines are short and give a concise rhyme; the penultimate line is long, giving a bathos or understatement in the final short line.

Try to list names and find easy rhymes, then build on that. Milton/Stilton, Disraeli/really, Mussolini/fettucini and so on. Then work on a longer line that is perky, bouncing along with a positive comment on the person's achievement. The only way is to practise.

AVOIDING THE OBVIOUS

Someone very helpfully invented a book which supplies rhymes for poets: a **rhyming dictionary**. Just as the great song-writers had to be inventive in finding rhymes for virtually any word, however unusual, so you will have to give your rhymes the maximum impact. There is nothing so dull in poetry as the monotonous, seemingly endless rhythms that never surprise or entertain. It is possible to learn a few techniques that increase your chances of maintaining the interest.

Follow the cadences of talk

Modern poets tend to think in terms of either performance or of a heightened version of the way we speak 'in code' – indirectly. Ask yourself how often you actually say what you mean. The art of everyday talk involves a constant dialogue: how to talk to the variety of people you meet in an average day. That is, you put on a 'performance', and that verbal dexterity is a sound basis for poetry. For instance, lines such as, 'What could I say? I was up a cul-de-sac' might be a fairly ordinary expression, but it has a rhythm, a way of emphasising that has poetic potential. The trick is to change word order: 'A cul-de-sac cried in every word I said.'

Change the norm

The idea of word order is very useful. In English, most sentences have a word order that follow this process of thought: subject–verb–object. For example, 'Paul saw his son – Paul = subject, saw = verb and son = object. This norm can be messed around creatively. Suppose you have a line in ordinary prose:

> *I felt that this was going to be the hardest test*

This could be changed to:

> *I tested the feelings that were hard inside*

and so on until you find a line that seems right.

Nouns to verbs

Shakespeare shows the way here. In *Anthony and Cleopatra* he talks about the captive Cleopatra being 'windowed' in Rome. He uses this instead of 'displayed'. He changes a noun to a verb. You can do this. For example, take this line from your prose journal, after seeing steelworks by night:

> *The hiss of steam and the red clouds of dust . . .*

This could be changed in this way:

> *Dust clouded and hissed by a steam-breathing beast.*

This is all worthwhile 'workshop' time, in which you can absorb a range of necessary language skills.

CASE STUDIES

Sue doesn't try too hard

Sue found her forte as a writer when she wrote satire. She had a knack for writing a neat, witty remark about someone. At first, her short, comic rhymes were printed in a local newspaper. Then she submitted to regional and thematic anthologies. She was pleased, but the difficulty was in writing something more sustained, ambitious – something longer!

Rhyming couplets were perfect. She read the best examples from modern poetry, including Sir John Betjeman, W. H. Auden, Roger McGough and others. None of these seemed to be in *her* idiom. Someone suggested that she read them aloud, to see if the spontaneity came across when she had an 'audience' – her two neighbours who encouraged her hobby.

Sue found that the sense of *having* to come up with a good rhyme generally worked. At last, she had something and she could develop the lines and rhythms later. She wrote a poem of ten couplets, after much drafting and editing.

Jim speaks in monologues

In his creative writing unit on his degree course, Jim discovered that writing about people 'from the inside' in the manner of Alan Bennett, was what he wanted to do most of all. Stories with conventional plots and 'twist in the tail' endings did not interest him; he preferred poetry and asked his lecturer for examples to read. The famous examples were, he discovered, by the Victorian poet, Robert Browning.

Jim found Browning hard going, but he persevered and he realised that the challenge was to make it read aloud 'naturally' – whatever that meant in terms of the writing skills. Yet also you had to be 'poetic' in all important qualities.

The lecturer's advice was to write in prose first, and then keep to free verse. To write in rhyme was totally unsuitable to what the lecturer referred to as 'interior monologue'. Jim had to become the speaker – to research the work that the character did and so on. It was like being an actor preparing for a role. But the monologue in free verse really succeeded. He wrote three for his assessed portfolio, and publication in the college magazine was just the beginning for Jim as a poet.

DISCUSSION POINTS

1. Why is it possible to 'learn' humour in poetry? Give some reasons why and how such skill or craft can actually be absorbed and written.

2. Suggest some types of poetic composition that would be unsuited to the use of rhyme.

6
Going into Print

KNOWING THE MARKETS

Why do you want to see your poetry printed? This may seem to be a pointless question, but it is important to ask yourself, once you have written a lot of poetry, why publish? There are some very basic reasons why people publish poetry:

● Vanity and satisfaction.

● To make money.

● To gain a reputation with your peers: critical esteem.

Ask yourself which of these applies to you. Of course, in writing there is always vanity. It gives you a thrill to see your name in print. The questions are, though, where and why and how?

A general trend
Many contemporary poets have a career development that follows a familiar pattern. These are the phases:

– **phase one**: publication in small magazines

– **phase two**: periodic but small-scale publication in larger magazines

– **phase three**: radio broadcasts and anthology publication

– **phase four**: the first collection – a slim volume from a small press.

Alongside this might come local readings, involvement with

regional magazines and so on. Only a very few are ever published by a large London or well-established regional publisher. The competition is intense and is growing all the time. The eventual first collection is most often from a small press or even self-publishing, but at the beginning, the first objective should be the small specialist magazines.

So what are the markets for poetry in terms of magazines? These are the main categories:

● literary magazines – with small circulation

● London-based magazines

● newspapers

● other magazines that use poetry as 'fillers'.

You need to get to know these markets. How is this done? First of all, be a regular visitor to bookshops and libraries. Make a note of any *new* magazines that take poetry and also which *established* magazines need a steady flow of poetry. Note which type of poetry is generally published. The details of all established magazines are in the standard reference books listed at the back of this book.

You can also join mailing lists to be up-dated on publishers, join local groups, send for free information about activities and so on. This is all a strategy for keeping informed and up-to-date. It can be a slow process, so make it easier for yourself by recording all this data systematically. Always have a notebook, and then transfer details into an index-book on your desk. The main points to bear in mind about markets for poetry are:

● they change rapidly

● they follow fashions

● they are often in need of 'names' to sell copies

● they rarely give you free criticism.

The following imaginery situation illustrates what is involved in getting to know your market. You have noted a county magazine that publishes three or four poems every month. Most of the magazine is devoted to local history and personalities, but half-pages or third-pages have poems. You read and study the type of poem required and the general subject-matter. Often this is the type of poetry you write naturally, but there is no reason why you cannot write for that specific outlet. After all, Roger Woddis used to write a poem every week in the *Radio Times*, commenting on a current issue.

LEARNING FROM THE EXPERTS

Professionals or seasoned campaigners in the poetry business often use the following methods to give themselves every chance of publication in magazines and similar outlets:

● get to know editors and their aims/tastes

● find all markets for their own speciality – even markets abroad

● research in literary weeklies and monthlies for new magazines

● up-date a file on local and national outlets for work

● send cards and CV to prospective editors with example of any previous work.

This might seem like an immense task, but eventually it becomes a habit as you organise yourself as a professional. If you are serious about your writing it is an essential part of the business. Records, reference books and local contacts always pay off. There are several other sources of potential publication once you start to network and become more involved in the poetry markets and the arts groups in your area.

It is essential also to consider the opposition. Competition now in the poetry scene is intensive, and the impact of the media on this is something that you should register realistically, and use to your advantage. For instance, consider these points:

● The media create a poet in terms of entertainment, not 'depth'.

● You can begin small-scale (local readings, radio) and grow from there.

- Without a hallmark, a distinctive identity, you sink.

- No-one helps *you* but yourself.

- Self-belief can achieve a lot.

DEVELOPING WORKING RELATIONSHIPS WITH EDITORS

You will soon learn that you need to get to know the editors of poetry magazines. Consider first what the editor of a small poetry magazine has to do and what the average magazine is like. A small magazine for example, has a circulation of a few hundred. This is the local publication, produced by desktop publishing on average quality paper, with no expensive illustrations or photography. It may be simply thirty pages of poems: nothing else. Usually, however, they contain reviews of new poetry, short articles, a little humour and an editorial.

What the editor wants

More than anything else a small magazine needs **subscribers**. If you submit work to such a publication, you often receive a reply that suggests that your work has merit, but that you should subscribe and send some more work. The editor wants your money and your name on his subscription list. This may only be say £10 a year, but you cannot be widely published in several such outlets without paying a considerable sum. Even subscription does not guarantee publication. An editor might accept your money, give a kind response, but publish more well-known writers when his subscription list grows. So he or she wants a little esteem, a touch of status, and enough money to carry on publishing.

Therefore, your first task is to find the editors who genuinely care about new and talented poets. There are plenty of these editors around. Never be too cynical, but adopt a questioning attitude. When you do find a receptive editor, cultivate a positive relationship. This may be achieved in a number of ways:

- *First establish a rapport*: Send work but suggest that you might contribute reviews occasionally, or offer a feature article. Describe something you could offer more than a few lyrics.

- *Engender co-operation and involvement*: Why not suggest that

Dear Editor,

Would you please note the enclosed three poems which I am submitting for your consideration. Are any of these suitable and of sufficient interest for your magazine and your readers? They are part of a longer thematic collection on . . . . . (give subject).

I have been writing poetry for just over a year now, and have published poems in some small magazines. This is my first submission to you. A stamped, addressed envelope is included for your convenience.

Yours faithfully

John Smith

Fig. 1. An example of a short covering letter for a submission.

you organise a reading in your area to promote the work of the magazine? Editors need some kind of promotion as often as possible.

- *Developing the relationship*: A point comes when you perhaps feel that you need more, and that you should widen the horizon, but keep in touch with the editors of any publications you have been involved in.

Editorial demands

Another aspect of working with editors, particularly as you progress, includes correspondence about changing your work. An editor might request changes or even tell you directly that he will print a poem if you change some lines or even the title. This is completely your decision – *never* be pressurised into amending your work. Keep to your beliefs and personal tastes. Only edit and rewrite if you feel sure that you are bending to a superior judgement.

Also, when you receive proofs of poems, always do the corrections and return immediately. Even more important is good, constant

communication by telephone and letter – or even the Internet if you are so equipped.

FOLLOWING THE RIGHT SUBMISSION PROCEDURES

There are some important guidelines to know and adhere to that every writer should be aware of in this matter of submitting material to editors:

- always include a short covering letter (see Figure 1)

- always include a stamped, addressed envelope

- make your text clear and checked for basic English

- never provide too much background about the writing

- don't include an in-depth CV.

The editor wants to be able to read a few lines about you and about the work submitted. He or she doesn't really want the work to be stapled together either. The best method is to provide loose sheets paper-clipped and placed in a plain folder.

Question
Is it really possible to write poems for a particular market? Surely poetry is based on inspirations and emotion, not written to order?

Answer
It is sometimes, but not always possible. You have to ask yourself whether or not you have that facility in you of actually coming up with rhymes or witty statements that would have a sharp contemporary feel, or say something in a refreshing way. (Read John Hegley!)

MAINTAINING PROFESSIONAL STANDARDS

All the way through your writing career, you need to maintain professional standards of work and presentation. The best advice you could receive is that these standards should begin right from square one. Setting professional standards should include: good working practice, genuine self-assessment, a healthy respect for quality work and a readiness to learn from anyone at any time. It's worth looking at these in more detail.

Good working practice

This means taking care of details as you research and gather materials. It means having clear records and checking on quality. How can you be sure of objective views of your work? You need to have second opinions – and opinions that count for something. An editor is too busy to provide a critical service for needy authors. However, you will need help with the 'quality control' aspect of your writing, and this could involve:

● paying for a critical report on your work

● joining a writing group

● editing and revising quite ruthlessly

● comparing your work over a period of time.

Honesty and an objective stance are difficult to achieve, but it is essential for an author to take a long, frank look at work and be satisfied on quality. Generally, it seems to be the case that first drafts very rarely achieve that standard which you actually ask of yourself. A normal process is to write poetry in a surge of creative thinking, writing down everything, and then editing, deleting and so on.

Genuine self-assessment and respect for quality

The above comments are written from experience. It is all too easy to assume that the first impulse that led you to write some poetry is the central core of poetic experience and is somehow sacrosanct. The professional habit however, is to question every word. Ask yourself if every word *earns* its place in the totality of the poem. Note any *repetition, slackness, redundant expression*. The red editing pen should always be handy. You should have benchmarks of quality in the areas of writing that you try to produce, and you should use these as yardsticks for your own writing. A personal anthology of your favourite poetry is no bad thing, much as the poet W. H. Auden did in his *Commonplace Book*.

A readiness to learn

This really does mean a readiness to learn from anyone who you respect, regardless of whether they have published excellent poetry or not. Teachers, general readers, people in other trades – anyone with an open mind and honesty is valuable to you, because too many people will smile and say your work is fine because they don't care about quality and progress. There are plenty of sources here from which to learn:

- reviews of poets and poetry

- interviews with poets

- readings and performance

- peer-group assessment.

Always read and reflect on statements made by poets you admire about the craft of poetry. Always read, listen and compare other poets' practice with your own.

CASE STUDIES

Dave learns the hard way

Dave had noticed that a new magazine had started in a town quite near him. It seemed bright and full of vitality, aimed at students perhaps, with a stress on youth, on humour and entertainment. He also noticed that they were looking for new contributors. At college, his tutors had admired his creative writing and Dave had wanted to be published, to try to make a name for himself, at least in his area.

He submitted six poems to the editor and received an encouraging response. The letter said that the writing was good, but there was no room to include any in the next issue. Did he want to subscribe at £15 for three issues? Dave thought about this, and asked his friends in class what they thought. The question was – what would he gain from subscribing? It didn't guarantee any publication. It did however, show interest and hint to the editor that Dave wanted to carry on sending material for consideration. He subscribed.

A year later, after four attempts to have poems included, the magazine folded. He never heard from the editor again. Since that time, Dave has had to subscribe to one large, London-based magazine, just to keep informed about the poetry scene. That has been worth it, but Dave's friends worked out that he would have had to spend at least £50 to increase chances of success, using three small magazines at least.

Lucy invents a system

Lucy had been a member of a writing group for ten years. They were mostly prose writers – only Lucy and her friend Janet were poets. Together they decided to try to be published in some regional anthologies. A publisher was looking for poems on a theme – the past – and they decided to join forces and write a sequence of poems together, based on the lives of young mothers in the fifties, when rationing was still around and times were hard.

They decided that they needed a way of working. Lucy, a secretary, was naturally well-organised and came up with the idea of writing poems based on family photographs. She wrote three short poems and included the texts with the photos, then sent them to Janet. Janet did likewise and they made copies of everything before sending them to the publisher.

The publisher liked the novelty of the idea and they burst into print. It was something to talk about at the next group meeting!

DISCUSSION POINTS

1. Suggest some ways in which you could improve your chances of being promoted as a local writer.

2. What should you do when submitting work to a publisher?

7
Participating in Writers' Groups

REFLECTING ON WHY WRITERS JOIN GROUPS

Most towns have some kind of writers' circle or creative writing group, and it's not hard to think of what sort of categories these might fall into. You may find that a group could be based around a class in a college or at the Workers' Educational Association perhaps. It might be more difficult to determine why people join them. The most common reasons include the following:

- a need to have good feedback and responses to your work

- the social element: writing is a lonely occupation

- the 'feelgood factor' – a sense of identity

- a chance to widen markets and generally network

- to learn professional writing from those who have succeeded.

The various types of groups can offer these things, but maybe it is difficult to find all the items on the list in one group. A lot depends on how dynamic the group is. Some may consist of amateurs who simply want to read their work aloud every month and have positive feedback. This mutual 'stroking' is not a good idea. It is generally unproductive. A writer wants honest, constructive criticism so that development is possible.

Another group may actively develop events and promote its writers with vigour and enterprise. You should certainly ask yourself what is to be gained from joining a group, but it must be said that, after a fair trial, you should accentuate the positive and note exactly what worthwhile activities will open to you on joining.

Getting help from equals

Despite the above comments, the breadth of experience gathered together in one group is always to be welcomed. The members will mostly be ambitious for wider recognition. Keeping your name in print and your work being read is what counts in the end, and even if the group simply publishes a small-scale magazine of work, so what? You have nothing to lose. The chances are that there will be one or two members whose writing compares in some way to your own, and that increases your chances of gaining something really valuable from your time with the group.

CHECKING ON WHAT GROUPS DO

As a member of a group you will find an amazing range of activities are open to you, depending on how much time and energy the members have. This section looks at some typical activities:

Anthologies and magazines

Although **anthologies and magazines** are often only printed cheaply, they can, at the very least, circulate your work locally. Some groups however, publish extremely good quality work. For instance, the Humberside Writers' Association published a paperback anthology in 1994, *Under a Mackerel Sky*, which is laminated, on good quality paper, and includes poetry and fiction, with illustrations.

Local radio

A group can target a particular 'slot' on **local radio**, such as a weekly poetry programme. In fact, an enterprising group can suggest and plan a programme on creative writing. The work of Ian McMillan in South Yorkshire, demonstrates this. Radio is a medium with plenty of scope for innovative writing, even in such areas as verse drama or monologues. A group can develop writing around a theme, take a local issue and so on.

Competitions

Another growth area in recent years has been the establishment of the **poetry competition**. There are now dozens of respected national and regional competitions, with hundreds of other smaller-scale ones developed locally. Groups often write specifically for competitions, as these sometimes have stated topics to be written about. Not everyone can work in groups, particularly in poetry, but in a group, it is possible to do research and preparation that is impossible individually. For instance, why not do a series of interviews with members of the group, selecting events and experiences which are potential 'material' for poetry?

Critical sessions and workshops

Writing groups usually have a rota providing individuals with the opportunity to read work and receive feedback or for the group as a whole to write to a target or deadline and then for all to read completed work, receiving comments from the assembled writers. Whichever one is used, your work is commented on and suggestions made. If this is not for you, well no-one forces you to join in!

A workshop, on the other hand, is more directed to one topic or form, and is usually led by a writer. A writer may come as a guest speaker and lead a workshop on specific skills such as writing comic poetry or writing free verse.

Visits and fieldwork

In a really enterprising and vibrant group, you may find that visits are arranged to places specifically to prompt writing – about place, people, industries, past and present, photo-journalism and so on. You might, for instance, visit a museum, and use the guide's information or walkman commentary as potential writing material. Again, the idea here is to expand possibilities by sharing thoughts and approaches. No-one ever said that writing poetry had to be done in a garret, ignored by the world.

Talks and guest speakers

Local or regional writers' groups are the ideal place to arrange and attend talks by professionals or by part-time writers who specialise in one type or genre. As far as poetry is concerned, there is now, more than ever before, a circuit of festivals and literature events in all parts of Britain in which guest speakers and local groups can participate. A more likely occasion, though, will be the formal talk. What is to be gained from this? The obvious answers are that someone who has succeeded tells you *how* they did so, although there is no universal formula you can note down and follow. Other advantages of the formal talk include:

- a question time, where you can ask specific questions on technique

- research notes: where ideas come from

- methods of work – sources of ideas

- influences – suggestions on what to read.

   Clearly, no other poet has the answer to your individual needs as a poet, but there is common ground – issues about form, current trends and so on.

ACCEPTING CONSTRUCTIVE CRITICISM

Supposing you went on working, relentlessly writing on your own, believing that you were really writing excellent poetry and that the world could not resist you and your work – what would be the dangers? Naturally, the main ones would be ignorance, obscurity, being out of date, and writing for no recognisable audience *etc*. In fact, where poetry is concerned, as recent successes by well-read poets shows, communicating with contemporaries is crucial to success.

   Therefore, you need responses and feedback. The word 'criticism' tends to imply something negative, pulling something to pieces; a destructive undertaking. But this is not the case. Good criticism points out improvement, or potential improvement. A critical response might also comment on your subject-matter. Suppose you have written 20 poems about ships and seafaring men. There could be someone in Leeds or Liverpool who has done the same, only more originally. If you had known, you could have changed tack, or written on something else.

Awareness

Criticism, when properly received, is about **awareness**. It is about being informed and knowing what other writers are doing. You find your own subject, but it might not be the best for you. Why re-invent the wheel? Work on something else. You need to be aware of stylistic features too: matters concerning your language, your approach and the voice you have developed – its originality, its confidence and its contemporary feel.

How is this done?
In a group, you might find that a batch of scripts is passed around for comment, without names appended. Each member of the group reads

all the scripts and adds brief comments, plus and minus. No-one knows who has written what. Or perhaps the writers of each category of writing work together each week, simply reading and commenting on each others' work. This is not only more relaxed, but also means you are face-to-face and can press for more accurate accounts of suggested weaknesses.

All approaches should have one thing in common – a desire to show the positive, to stress what has been *achieved*. There is no point in arguing in terms of offended vanity. You have joined a group to learn, so accept that all learning is beneficial but also sometimes hard to take.

Rejection slips and group comments
Compare these two ways of finding out about what is poor in your poetry.

1. **The rejection slip**. An editor sends you a slip of paper with a typed statement something like this: 'Thankyou for submitting your work. I am afraid that it is not suitable for our publication.'

2. **The group criticism**. A few colleagues point out that line three is flat and spoils the poem. Work on that and it will be a stronger piece of writing.

It should be obvious why constructive criticism is so useful!

LEARNING BY REWRITING

As mentioned earlier, very few poems are written once and then left as complete, finished works of art. You will constantly have to rework and rewrite poems. There could be several reasons why revision is necessary:

● poor syntax – this could be weak expression, ambiguity *etc*

● redundancy or repetition: you need to cut words.

● wrong form or style

● grammatical errors/improved punctuation needed.

here is an example of a poem that had three earlier versions. It is called 'Anglers'.

> Silent, intent on the dream
> of a white-gold flash beneath them,
> the anglers tip their thoughts out
> like the wriggling bait
> on sodden earth . . .

This is only the first section of the poem, but it needed revisions. The first line was originally, 'The silent anglers dream', then it became 'Dreamily, the quiet anglers sit'. In other words, the first line need to be compact. The poem is simple, with a lot of meaning and imagery crammed into a short space. The end of the full poem compares fishing to writing:

> And I am jealous, as I fish for
> metaphors to beat the last one.
> See, it was this big, I swear.

The poem tries to link the pride of a 'catch' with the thrill of writing a superb image that gives the poet a feeling of achievement.

'I wish he had blotted a hundred'
Ben Jonson, writing about his friend Shakespeare, said that his work would have been better had it been edited, with cuts made, and so on. Even the greatest have had what was meant to be very constructive criticism from their friends.

Rewriting is in many cases very pleasurable and rewarding. It is a creative process in itself. When you reread the text of a poem, the weaknesses show, particularly when read aloud, and this is a useful habit to cultivate. Read aloud whenever possible. The weak joints show – a poem should read fluently and naturally.

Some rough guidelines
It is not possible to give all the examples of when rewriting may be necessary, but here are some of the most common weaknesses:

- **too many linking words** – note uses of 'and', but' *etc*, and edit where needed

- **too much like prose** – cut words to condense a full explanation

- **ambiguous** – test a poem on a listener to try its sense and clarity

- **repetitions** – do you tend to use the same word six times in twelve lines?

SETTING HIGH STANDARDS

What criteria are you to use as a poet? It is never too early to decide on what is acceptable to you. You might refer to certain exemplary 'models' in poems where you know that what you actually wanted to write is there on the page. Writers will often tell you that there is a huge gap between the feeling or idea that was in their head and the actual printed poem. That sense of having written on paper precisely what was in the mind is apparently quite rare in writing.

Possible benchmarks might be:

1.   Your favourite, most respected poet who writes on your subject.

2.   Your own most successful poem.

3.   A feeling that somehow you could do better.

Ideally, it would be wonderful if you could recognise the second-best as it is written, but this is rarely the case. You have to read widely and assess, to your own satisfaction, what the achievements of the successful poets in your time really are.

Question
Surely groups are never honest. Can I really expect an honest response to my poetry?

Answer
Only if you make it plain that you want a frank response. It is up to you to state the actual 'rules of the game' in critical response and interchange.

Seeing and knowing the best
In all varieties of literature, there is debate about what constitutes the best writing – what exactly the word 'best' means. But it should be easy to agree on some criteria. A poem must say something that

demonstrates insight and philosophic thought. It should stand more than one reading, it should outlast its time and be universal. The 'best' contains these qualities. So ask yourself (and others) whether your most successful poems qualify.

CASE STUDIES

Bill leads by example

Bill was sceptical about writing circles. He imagined that they would be mutual admiration societies and that people there would *talk* about writing but never actually do very much. But a friend of his was going along to test the ground, so Bill went with him.

At first, his suspicions seemed to be confirmed. About ten people sat around, sipping coffee and chatting. There seemed to be no organisation, no agenda. Then someone said that they should get their work out, report on progress and read a few extracts. Bill and his friend were invited to listen and comment if they felt like it.

One after another, the members read and talked. In fact, they talked more than they read. It seemed to be obligatory to spend a long time explaining the experience and the idea before getting down to reading the work. After half an hour, everyone had said quite a lot, and in fact some useful criticisms and suggestions had been made.

Bill was given a sheet summarising forthcoming events, given a task for the next meeting and introduced to the other aspiring poets in the group. He seized the moment and offered to organise a reading by the groups' poets at a future arts festival in a neighbouring town. Heads turned. They all saw a prospective member who would 'get things done'. Bill made his own involvement, and that was the point, he saw, about writers' groups.

Ruth pays for a report

In a writing magazine, Ruth, who wrote poetry exclusively, saw an advert from a writing school offering a critical report on any piece of writing. There was a fee of £40 and she wondered what she would receive for her money. After some thought, she decided to try it, because she was not getting any useful feedback from editors, and she was not being published. Why was she not good enough? Would she ever be good enough and was she wasting her time trying to be a poet if the skill was just not there?

The report came after about two weeks. She had sent six of what she thought were her best poems. The critic (a professional writer and tutor) pointed out that, despite a list of about ten critical notes, she should continue because her work showed talent. With that statement in writing, she could take the criticism. She carefully read all the comments and assessed their justness. It was hard to take at times, but Ruth saw for the first time how unquestioning she had been of her own work.

Steadily, more and more poems found publication. She had been working entirely on her own and had been producing inferior work due to lack of discussion and feedback.

DISCUSSION POINTS

1. What would be some suitable activities for a writers' group if it wanted to participate in a literature festival? List some possibilities.

2. How could a magazine, written and produced by a group, be promoted locally? List and describe some ideas and activities.

8
Going from Poems to Collections

DEFINING THE IDEA OF A COLLECTION

This is the ultimate dream: to have a collection of your own. Why is this so important?

1. It is a mark of achievement.

2. It is a landmark in your career.

As you progress as a poet, your manuscript collection will grow. You will perhaps have a file of poems that have been worked on but never completed; some will have been finished but you were never pleased with them so they remain unsubmitted. Then there will be the poems you feel have succeeded. It is from this resource file that you should start to think about submitting to a publisher in terms of your first full collection. There will be different groupings in your mind within this file also. It is useful to sort out all your mass of typescripts and manuscript poems into these categories if you are at the stage of planning a collection:

- poems which are not to be further developed

- poems which are finished but have not been shown or submitted

- poems published in magazines or broadcast *etc.*

From the last category, sort into subjects and/or styles. Most poets have ongoing themes which they write about in different ways as they improve and change. The fundamental question is whether or not you have the basis of a good, strong collection with a number of poems that come over well to the reader. If you have about 30 to 40 poems that could form a thematic collection, then sort these into the following categories:

- a rank order imposed by your own sense of which are most successful

- sets, groups or sequences by topic or style

- variety – of length, narrative device and so on.

There is always a rationale behind a successful collection. What defines a collection then? You will see some books on the poetry shelves that seem to be a random group of 40 poems all on different subjects and written in different ways. Some publishers do simply want to produce a collection from a writer because they consider it to be the right time, and because people will read anything if they know the name of the author through media hype and good advertising.

There are several aspects of the planning to consider:

- Have most of the poems been published in magazines or anthologies?

- Is there a factor which helps them all to be unified in the reader's mind?

- Is there a persistent tone or attitude in them, stemming from yourself?

When that is sorted out, reflect on what types of publisher exist. There is the London scene, which is a mixture of large publishers such as Faber and smaller ones, often depending on Art Council grants for their existence. Then there are the small presses, all with varying agendas and sources of finance. There will also be a considerable range of quality on offer in terms of the presentation and format of your projected book. Marketing and distribution will be difficult for all small presses. The challenge begins to open up.

LOCATING YOUR OWN THEME AND STYLE

Basically, a poet wanting to break into print with a collection needs to be sure that the venture springs from a sound base of achievement. You need to define who you are and build up a name. Your aim is to make sure that some publishers will have heard of you before you submit. Not many aspiring poets achieve this, so note and plan the following stages of development, and how to secure them.

Stage one: broadcasting your image

The poetry scene now is not for shy types. The most prominent change has been in the burgeoning of performance poetry. The pop culture of the sixties and the links made between song lyrics and poems in the Bob Dylan/Beatles era, together with recent cabaret and performing arts developments, has meant that the successful poet is the public one. The success of such writers as Benjamin Zephaniah, John Cowper Clarke, Roger McGough and John Hegley testifies to the fact that a slim volume is not enough. You need an image. So, offer to participate in radio programmes in your area. Do readings whenever you can. Work in schools with poetry workshops. Start a small magazine. **Keep doing something that keeps your name current in people's minds**.

Stage two: networking your writings and your image

Again, reticence will not win success. Distribute examples of your work, a CV and a business card to all publishers, together with a representative sample of your poetry. Any editors who give you an encouraging response should be written to or phoned as soon as possible. Use the regional arts council and find out about grants for writers.

Stage three: starting with a small press

Many well-known poets first published in pamphlet form with a small press. These can be either a cheap ten-page booklet or a well-produced fifty-page book. However, a small press publication will not receive much reviewing space and will not usually be distributed very well, so your book will only be read by a minority – and by your friends.

Stage four: trying the big fish

You are now at the point of being a big fish in a small pond. When you have a sound written record of achievement and have gained status in the poetry scene you can approach the large publishers with more assurance.

This all sounds so perfect, the ideal route upwards and forwards. In fact, it is difficult to achieve, but you have to *try* if you genuinely wish to succeed as a poet. Too many writers dream and wait for a miracle. You have to make things happen in today's business-led world.

Defining your style

You can see from the above that your **theme and style** are not simply in the poems on the page. They are an integral part of *you* – your personality. If you separate the two, you decrease the chances of success for that first collection.

APPROACHING PUBLISHERS

This first collection is the sign of your arrival in the poetry world. Many poets never achieve this, despite the fact that their work is circulated in dozens of magazines and anthologies. So maximise your chances of success by thinking carefully about your submission. These are the steps to take:

Choose your publisher

Study the publishers' lists and also look closely at the current *Writers and Artists' Yearbook* and *The Writers' Handbook* (see reading lists at the end of the book) and look at as many volumes as you can from the publishers which seem to be most suited to your type of poetry. There tend to be these categories of poetry, each with their own particular specialist publishers:

- traditional verse with a rural, English subject area

- experimental – promoting 'concrete' poetry *etc*

- specialist – publishing poetry about one topic *eg* science fiction/ fantasy

- local – only interested in poetry about a specific region

- theoretical – interested in poetry following a 'party line'.

You can see from this just how much care you need to take here. You could waste a large sum of money packing off your typescript to publishers who would never publish you simply because you write differently from their norm.

Once you have found a publisher who seems to publish poetry

similar to yours, then compile a covering letter about yourself, with a CV and list main magazine-based publication you have achieved, together with any broadcast or anthologised work and other related details. The following is a full checklist of what may be relevant to your submission:

- CV

- activities – workshops and performances given

- publications/broadcasts

- a summary of the themes you generally write about

- writers' groups you are involved in.

Finally, it is worth reminding yourself of the obvious courtesies involved in a professional submission:

- a stamped, addressed envelope

- sheets numbered and not permanently bound

- scripts enclosed in a plain folder

- lists of poems previously published, stating your ownership of copyright.

RESEARCHING THE SMALL PRESSES

Think about the nature of a **small press** and research what they want from writers. A small press may be in one of several categories: most often it produces two or three books a year, operates on a tight budget and is the centre of a one-person enthusiastic enterprise. There may be funding with a dependence on a certain number of subscribers. Even more frustrating for a poet sending a collection to an unknown from an unknown is the fact that there is no clear statement of the 'policy' of the press. There may be no catalogue, either, to give potential contributors an idea of what is published.

With all this in mind, this should be your procedure:

1. Read the reference books

Read the chapter on small presses and check the list of small poetry presses in Barry Turner's handbook (see Further Reading). The small presses are well described, and from Turner you will gain an impression of whether or not they would be likely to have an interest in your material. The poetry presses are more problematic:

1. Some presses have no statement as to their preferences.

2. There are a number of specialist presses such as Enitharmon and Arc.

3. Some presses run a magazine as well and this is a helpful guide.

2. Send for examples

At this point, it will cost a few pounds to see and study typical publications from the number of presses you have selected. What is important is that you submit to the specialist poetry presses first. The investment on specimen books is worth it, as you could spend even more on postage to the wrong presses, and this also delays the whole process.

3. Write an explanatory letter if in doubt

If the press has published something very recently, and it stands comparison with your own work, then it is the right time to submit, but if they have not published anything for more than a year, make enquiries by letter to make sure they are receptive to a submission. Circulation figures may be quoted in Turner for the specialist presses, but not for the small ones. You have no idea about the costs involved and you may be asked to contribute funds.

Quality

A factor in all this which is often a last thought is the **quality** of the finished product. The excitement of contemplating your first collection in book form may override basic details such as what the presentation and format of the eventual book will be. This is where your original research comes in useful. There is a range of widely-used formats for such poetry volumes:

●   laminated cover and well-printed texts

- card cover

- desk-top quality but thin card or even paper cover

- pamphlet form, stapled

- bound/spiral.

In addition to this, the quality of the paper and the durability are important. The overall image should of course be attractive, but it should also be strong enough to endure plenty of use. The first on the above list, the laminated cover, is the crucial element here. A glossy look with a powerful and relevant cover illustration, are the most vital considerations.

Question
Are you wasting time and money submitting to a publisher if you have published very little and are simply offering 40 poems which are mostly unpublished?

Answer
Almost always, yes. Few publishers would venture into print with a complete 'unknown'. The more work you have had published in magazines or anthologies, or had broadcast, then the higher your chances of acceptance. But you could be a genius! There are no absolutes here.

VANITY PUBLISHING

In several daily papers and in hundreds of other publications, you will often see adverts for presses who offer to publish your poetry. They will not mention the fact that you have to pay a large amount of money to see your work in print. In some cases, the finished volume would be excellent: a hardback with a wonderful gold-lettered spine. But it costs a great deal and who would read it? It would not be reviewed in poetry magazines and the event would go unnoticed by everyone except you and your friends.

Why pay a publisher?
There is only one answer to this: **desperation**. The only good thing

to come out of this is the satisfaction of putting a book on the shelf with your name on the spine. Even if you sold copies at readings, you would never recoup the costs. Note the distinction between **vanity publishing** and **self-publishing**:

vanity: A company oversees the whole process. No involvement from you except when you sign the cheque.

Self: You invest in the venture, and are involved in the planning, design and distribution. It is possible to make a profit if you think it through properly (see Chapter 10).

You will sometimes see volumes produced by vanity presses, but that is a rare event. In most cases, they are not represented by a distribution company. Such expenditure would not represent any investment in your career as a poet. So beware of any announcement on the lines of **'Your book published: do you have a masterpiece in your drawer?'** and similar selling lines.

CASE STUDIES

John finds cooperation

John had been writing poetry for ten years. He had made a modest local reputation for himself by having poems broadcast on the local radio, doing work in schools and generally being active in artistic and literary events. He had retired early from industry, had always enjoyed writing in his spare time, but now he needed to make it more central in his life. Looking around, he saw that you needed to have a book 'to your name'. The Arts Council for his county published a directory of writers, and he had his name put into this, the idea being that he could find work in schools and with adult groups, to earn a little money.

The other writers in this directory all seemed to have published a book. You could find their work in the library, and John realised that if and when he did workshops with groups, a book of his own would lend prestige. He realised that vanity presses and self-publishing would mean considerable outlay, so was there another way? He read about cooperative publishing and that led to his first step: a share in a book with two other writers.

The result was a book with three names on the cover, and his was one of them. It was almost a book of his own. The real advantage of this, though, was that he could sell copies at readings and workshops. By assiduously putting aside all earnings from sales and from readings, in a year he had enough finance to produce a book of his own.

Linda writes a writer's CV

All the handbooks about writing success pointed it out – you needed a CV specifically for your writing and you should up-date it every few months. Linda had published widely. She was a minor 'name' in the north of England and the time was right to publish. Even more exciting was the fact that she had a small bursary from an Art Association award scheme. She had enough finance and status to attract a small press with some quality writing on its lists.

The question was what to include on this CV. It was someone at her writing circle who helped her – a business person with lots of experience in public relations, and that was something that Linda had never been much good at. She just wrote under these headings;

● poems in magazines

● poems in anthologies

● broadcast work

● workshops and reading (chronological order)

● awards, bursary and competitions

● references from professionals.

It all looked very impressive. Certainly the publisher was impressed. A good, well-reviewed collection followed. Without some help from someone with experience, it would have been far more difficult. Linda realised from this that she had been far too much the 'dreamy' artistic type – and now she was determined to get organised.

DISCUSSION POINTS

1. How could you tell, from a reference book, which small presses took an interest in your kind of poetry?

2. Suggest some ways of organising poems around a theme, going from a file of work to a well-defined collection.

9
Researching Wider Markets

NETWORKING FOR ANTHOLOGIES

At a point when you have reached the stage of submitting a collection, contemplate some moves to broaden your scope. There is often
a stage in a poets development when they have achieved a certain
reputation but are still having to work hard to find print. The letters
asking for contributions do not often come to them and they still have
to do all the pushing. The reason is, of course, that there is so much
competition. So what potential routes are there for increasing your
options?

Starting a business operation

No-one will notice your talents if you don't display them. There have
been too many writers who have been convinced that being published
in small magazines is enough to launch into a career. The majority
will never be 'discovered'. Ask yourself whether London publishers
are likely to read small poetry magazines in order to find new talent
when they already receive dozens of collections from hopefuls and
wannabes every week. You need to operate John Smith, Poet, as a
business – but how?

1. Circulate examples of your work to anthologists.

2. Get involved in promotion events with your local arts
   association.

3. Keep in the public eye.

4. Most of all, constantly find new markets and outlets.

The last one is the crucially important step to take, but the first step
towards this is to try to have poems considered for anthologies.

Dozens of publishers have a running project of keeping a few school poetry anthologies on the shelves, and sales to schools can be quite considerable. Where do they gather material for these anthologies? Obviously, they can write to well-known names, but there is always a chance for the newcomer if the work is good enough.

Submissions need to be contemporary

There are three steps towards anthology publication:

1. Write a standard letter and circulate to all publishers who tend to produce anthologies.

2. Submit only poems that match their usual themes and formats.

3. Send a selection of six to ten poems.

Clearly, as the main readership is to be schoolchildren, research the market first. What do children of a specific age-group read and enjoy? To maximise your chances of success, you should:

●   write in strongly contemporary language

●   inject humour – gentle satire, irony where possible

●   be accessible – select every word as a working word

●   don't be 'literary'.

USING GROUPS AND COMPETITIONS

Recently, there has been a real mushrooming of poetry groups, both large and small, all there to help members find publication outlets. Most of these can be of undeniable benefit to you. They offer the chance to network; to find out about which editors are looking for what sort of material or subject-matter and so on. There tends to be a range of categories here, but the really useful and worthwhile ones are cooperatives. The group publishes its own magazine and has a critical service for members, small grants and a system by which poets who have slowly gathered a number of quality poems can be helped to form a collection.

Editors and anthologies: smaller scale

Outlets for publication can also be found through smaller publishers who aim at thematic collections or at regional areas. Profits are not massive, but you do see your work in print. One of the largest of these is *Poetry Now* and its related press. The aim is to publish a large number of poets in each anthology and pay a small royalty or give a donation to charity from the moderate sales. However, these books are well-circulated and distributed and your work has a good chance of being read.

Competitions: a success story

Other poetry groups survive by means of organising poetry competitions. Most libraries now are well stocked with leaflets announcing a competition held by a poetry group. These are worth the small investments involved and there are some interesting developments in this area.

1. The pamphlet collection

This is a competition organised in such a way that a certain number of winners have a pamphlet of their best poems printed as their prize. The entry fee is usually around £10, but the prize is a chance to get into print in a way that will have some impact.

2. Cash prize and publication

Here, your poem will be printed in a specific magazine if it wins a prize, and there will be a cash prize. There is obviously some kudos associated with this, as you are included, in most cases in a prestigious literary magazine.

3. Festivals

Another feature of the poetry scene now is the prominence of contemporary poetry in the literature festivals throughout the year. Poetry competitions linked with festivals have the great advantage that the winning poems are read at a place with a guaranteed and enthusiastic audience. Again, there is a high level of media attention here and more chance of your work being noticed.

FINDING MARKETS ABROAD

The standard reference books on poetry markets all draw attention to the fact that many poets never consider submission to magazines and publishers abroad. It is easy to settle into a circuit of well-known out-lets and editors, together with your familiar subjects and themes. There is nothing wrong with this, but it does ignore some potential expansion.

The books which list markets in the USA for instance, point to a vast market in a country which has an explosion of poetry and much more potential for growth than many other places. Magazines from groups and societies will always be looking for poets from other roots who are writing about other cultures. There are also the mainline American publications on the news-stands in London and the literary journals, and the latter are the best place to start. Journals published by universities, and poetry publications for new writers always have a high profile.

The importance of research

Naturally, you need to look carefully at what exists and at what has been established for a long time. The drawback is that it is not easy to have access to example issues. The easiest way is to visit a university library periodicals section and check on the American magazines, but the standard books listed in the Further Reading section at the end of the book do describe the publications well.

Question
The problem with anthologies is that they don't sell widely and don't appear in many bookshops. Is it worth all the effort and expense?

Answer
Yes, definitely. Your name and work will be read by editors, who receive feedback from teachers and other professionals *etc.*

READINGS, PERFORMANCES AND WORKSHOPS

Ask yourself what kind of poet you are:

1.   The reticent type who writes for personal satisfaction.

2.   The type who feels passionately about issues and people.

3. The type who absolutely *must* communicate to others *now* and forcefully.

This is an important question because poetry now is a part of the repertoire of performance. Since the impact of the Mersey Poets in the sixties, there has been an increasing tendency for poetry to come out of the garret and into the public arena. When your first collection is published, or when you are known locally as a writer, you may be asked to give a reading. Equally, you need to think about whether performance is part of your involvement with the art of poetry.

Why read or perform?

There are many reasons, but the most significant one is the drama of it. A reading is a presentation of your poetry: a delivery, with a certain voice and stance. You display yourself and your poetic persona to a public just as much as a singer or a stand-up comedian. One of the most skilled performers and readers of poetry in England, Ian McMillan, mixes poetry with anecdotes and above all with his expression of his personality. Once you have decided that you would like to promote your work by reading, you have a choice between two basic approaches to the job:

1. **Read quietly and give a short commentary on each poem**. The focus is then intensely on the words that make up the poem's structure.

2. **Perform: bring your personality to the fore**. Here, the words, the 'music' of your rhythms, is shown as a part of who you are and why you write.

Clearly, such events involve payment and you do sell copies of your book, but readings vary from a reading to a thriving poetry group with 30 people attending, to a village hall where a handful of people have asked you to come along because they have a vague interest in anything literary and you come cheap.

Workshops: what are they?

Again, as a promotional manoeuvre, a workshop can be fruitful and very worthwhile. Usually, the term means that you read work but guide others into writing also, perhaps on a theme or in a certain style. You might hold a workshop for a class in adult education and talk about writing comic poetry or religious poetry and so on. You might give a 'one-off' workshop on metrical poetry and read or discuss examples.

Common varieties might be classed in this way:

- in schools or colleges, as part of a course

- in conjunction with literary events

- locally, as a means of involving people in writing skills.

You should prepare very carefully for any of the above promotional steps, and be sure that you have researched the audience's needs and tastes. But in the end, any element of performance and delivery in poetry involves a developing sense of what you wish to project and why. You only learn by doing, and the rewards are tremendous. You have instant acclaim and response; feedback in discussion is fulfilling and exciting and of course, your ego has a good time. Also, all this will look impressive on a CV or submission.

USING ARTS ASSOCIATIONS

The regional arts associations exist for many reasons, but one aspect of their work which is to your advantage is the encouragement of literature. Each one has to finance enterprises in fiction, drama and poetry, in addition to groups, publications and festivals. Some funds will be allocated to writing in schools, perhaps, or to community projects. You can certainly apply for help as a struggling poet. The options are:

1. Apply for a grant or bursary for a project.

2. Be involved in a scheme to bring poetry to the people *etc*.

3. Promote arts events by publication or education and ask for finance.

The arts associations like to think that their funding to literature helps to initiate something with a chance of permanence, such as a writers' group or an annual festival or competition.

Before you submit your application to your regional arts

association it might be useful to consider whether it meets any of the following criteria:

1. Does your plan involve the community actively?

2. Is there an aspect of regional identity?

3. What part does your own skill and writing play in this?

4. What help is available to you?

Some examples of innovative and worthwhile schemes have been a 'write a poetry book day' involving a workshop where people of all ages write and assemble an anthology; a writing session in which photography was used to monitor social change in a community; and an oral history project involving poetry and prose about the lives of senior citizens.

CASE STUDIES

Cathy is big in the States

Cathy had been publishing in small magazines for about five years when she came to the realisation she was stuck. There seemed to be no possibility of progress in the poetry world, as she could not find any response in the offices of the larger, cosmopolitan poetry magazines, who always rejected her work, politely. One journal had rejected her poems on five occasions, each time being 'encouraging'. She needed to branch out.

The *Writers' and Artists' Yearbook* listed some magazines that were interested in new contributors' work, and she sent off six poems to three of these. To her amazement, the editors were captivated by her originality! Her whole tone and approach were so novel and refreshing to the editor of one of the publications, that she took three of the poems immediately and wanted to see more work.

After a few years, Cathy was appearing in anthologies. Her work was actually reviewed in some smaller magazines, and she felt that she had arrived. It was simply the careful reading of a standard reference book (one she has previously only skimmed) that helped her. She had been resisting change because she felt inferior, too provincial and limited in range. But another culture found her range to be quite different and innovative in approach.

Jim goes public

Jim was doing incredibly well in his business since he took early retirement – so much so that he had some cash available to try what he had always wanted to do – to be involved in poetry and literature in some way. He had studied marketing as a necessity, but writing had always been his first love. He had several options, but one was to start a small press. He bought a desk top publishing set-up and started to publish booklets of poetry. He was never short of writers.

Yet he wanted to do more. The booklets of poetry were fine, but they tended to be written by poets for poets, and he had always thought that writing should be enjoyed by anyone – 'literary type' or not. The solution was to start some public events, and everywhere you looked there seemed to be a reading or a performance.

He hired a room in a hotel, invited some of his 'in-house' poets to work out a programme, and started promoting the events. Never in his wildest dreams did he envisage what would happen. The project went from strength to strength. He was soon in a position to invite more well-known poets, and the whole thing gained something of a reputation.

Jim himself started reading – and that was the greatest triumph, as he had a sense that there really was an audience, not just a mutual admiration society admiring each others' slim volumes of verse.

DISCUSSION POINTS

1. How might you make a start in the performance and readings 'circuit'? What would be the best type of approach to arts associations *etc*?

2. Suggest some ways in which you might plan and finance your own thematic or regional anthologies.

10
Considering Self-Publishing

WHY USE THIS OPTION?

Self-publishing can mean two things: either publishing your own book by yourself, with desk top publishing facilities or paying a company to do this for you. Either way, the principle is the same – **you are financing the enterprise**. Why would you do this? You might have been rejected by several publishers but still believe in yourself and that your writing has merit. It is helpful here to summarise the features of the two approaches:

Publishing the book yourself

This means that you have to use your own printing facilities to produce a professional text. You have to be all these things and more:

* market researcher

* paper buyer

* computer operator

* typographer

* copy-editor

* illustrator.

And so it goes on. So this option is only for those who have the finance to invest in a full desktop publishing package, including a scanner and quite sophisticated illustration input. In other words, for most of us, self-financed publishing is probably the best option – if we are talking about really good quality production.

However, anyone with a personal computer can produce a decent booklet, perhaps paying for the lamination of the cover and for the binding, but doing the layout and pagination oneself.

Paying a company to publish

Isn't paying a company to publish your book the same as vanity publishing? In a way it is but not in the sense described earlier. The point about this is that you pay some specialists, but the text is done by you, and you control distribution, even if most of that is simply local. You might consider these factors if you want to try this option:

- Start small: print say 200 copies of a stapled booklet.

- Sell locally through bookshops and readings.

- Send copies for review to magazines.

- Do the cover yourself – laminate if possible.

The point is, **make a start**. If you finance it yourself but do the presentation according to what you personally prefer, then you have a text that you feel good about.

Guidelines
Think about these aspects of the presentation and even a card-covered booklet can be impressive and give you a headstart.

1.   Do you want illustrations?

2.   What font is most suitable?

3.   What about borders and pagination?

4.   Cover design – a line drawing or a photograph?

You might find that some of this is possible but that some of it is beyond you. Why not enlist the help of students at a local college? Art students are always looking for interesting projects. Contact the tutor of an art and design course and describe your project. The college will welcome the potential 'good press' it would gain from the enterprise.

Your best move, though, in the first place is to study what exists already and estimate what range of formats and quality is viable for you and your resources.

CONSIDERING SOME EXAMPLES OF SUCCESS

There are three notable types or formats which represent the possibilities for you here:

1. The stapled booklet

I have in front of me a booklet of A5 size, with 48 pages and a card cover. The 48 pages have 42 pages of poems. There are no illustrations, and the cover has a line drawing. It is not laminated. It is available from the author, as the inside cover tells me. You might be able to buy it in a few local bookshops, and it is sold in the local library, displayed in a glass cabinet of local publications, besides works on local history.

Advantages	*Disadvantages*
The writer is known locally.	The distribution is poor.
Small magazines might review.	No larger publishers would know
The author might sell directly.	about it.
The author has control.	Few people will notice the book.
	Large bookshops will not stock it.

2. Bound and laminated

This costs you more, as you need to pay a local printer or small press to heat-bind and laminate. Also, the cover illustration needs colour for maximum effect.

Advantages	*Disadvantages*
The product looks classy.	It is still only local distribution.
There is more chance of	It is still not likely to compete for
being noticed.	space with Faber or other large
You have control.	publishers.
	You will need specialists – more
	costs.

3. The small press does everything

Imagine a one-man small press with literary interests. They have the facilities and the technology to produce books of excellent quality. The owner will produce your book at no cost to you. You can keep the copyright, but the printer needs the sales income. You can get all the quality described above, with the bonus of photo-images done by computer technology if you wish.

Advantages	Disadvantages
You can still be involved in the creation.	It costs more.
	The printer has to pay for distribution.
You work with an enthusiast.	
Marketing is possible.	Marketing still costs.
There are more chances of being noticed.	This needs promotion and time.

With all these options in mind, the final choice is still the same – quality and costs are important but distribution leads the whole adventure. **You want as many people as possible to buy and read your book**.

COSTING THE PROCESS AND PROMOTION

In the publishing described above, profit is not the main motive. You want to circulate your poetry. But the book should still sell, and you want to at least break even. Aiming at a local market, using your contacts, increases your chance of guaranteed sales, particularly if you give readings from the book to local groups. If you multiply production costs by five, then to sell about 700 out of a print run of 1200 would regain your expenses. Anything else is a profit. Of course, poetry has a limited market anyway, and you should only print a few hundred.

Considering worthwhile losses

1. Copies sent for review – loss.

2. Copies given to professionals for promotion – loss.

3. Reductions in price after poor sales – loss.

The problem with poetry is that it only sells if energetically backed. Your local W.H. Smith is invaluable here, and Smith's does tend to be buying more small-press stock with local interest.

This level of publishing is small, so there is no need to register for

VAT, or to claim expenses based on a first-year loss. However, there are cases of small publishers who have begun with love and enthusiasm and then moved to quite considerable sales and status.

Assessing the outlay

Even on the small-scale level of a heat-bound booklet of say 30 pages, you might need to spend this:

- binding and photocopying/reduction – £40 average for 100 copies

- photograph or colour – 80p per image per issue!

- costs of flyers, leaflets, local press adverts

- free copies for review.

Promotion

This is in your hands, and you can make or break the business by not preparing thoughtfully. The potential points of sale are:

- readings

- workshops

- local shops

- direct to writing groups

- in other local shops and cafes

- museums and libraries.

Self-promotion

Self-promotion involves **research** and **networking** for contacts. You must have a wide range of contacts if you are at the stage in your writing career when you have published in magazines and anthologies and perhaps broadcast your work. Here is a checklist of potential contacts:

The local scene

– librarians
– arts officer for the council
– the arts association literature officer
– bookshop manager
– lecturers involved with adult groups.

The wider scene

– small press publishers
– magazine editors
– reviewers and critics
– administrators of events, grants, reading circuits *etc*.

What most poets in this situation would do is think small, local or regional. This is fine up to a point, but being different and being bold can bring quicker success. The real centrepiece of any poetry promotion should be a series of readings to groups. A large publisher will often organise this, and some have well-established venues and local contacts. You cannot compete with this, but you can use some contacts further afield. The best first move is to write to your regional arts association and to the nearest association of writers. They could offer you these potential promotional (and sales) opportunities:

● registry of you name in a writers' directory

● involvement in events such as writers' clinics, school workshops *etc*

● applications for grants for specific projects

● professional advice

● contacts locally.

The idea of a directory of writers was started, for example, by the Northern Association of Writers in Education (NAWE) some years ago, and is now up-dated regularly. You send a writer's CV to them and this is circulated so that if groups are interested, they will get in touch with you and set up an event.

Do a writer's CV

Your CV is something you should have up-dated and sent out at every opportunity to any potential contact or outlet for work. Figure 2 will give you an idea of the format it should take.

JOHN SMITH: POET

1. Born 1960, Sheffield. Educated, London University

2. Publications *etc.*

   (a) Poems in magazines (list)
   (b) Poems in anthologies (list)
   (c) Competition successes (list)

3. Broadcast work (details)

4. Readings and workshops done (details)

5. Current projects (details)

6. Activities offered and preferred age-groups *etc.*

7. Availability

8. Contact information

Fig. 2. Possible format for a CV.

You might have responses from schools, colleges, writing circles or even offers of involvement in literature festivals or courses. Regardless of what method you use, make it such that your name is memorable. Have a business card always available with your identity as a freelance writer/poet clearly prominent on the card and use a logo.

FINDING INFORMATION

There are four main easily-available sources here:

- reference books

- magazines for writers

- arts associations

- professional associations.

These each offer different kinds of information sources.

Reference books

The two standard reference books, as listed in the Further Reading section, are Barry Turner's *The Writer's Handbook* published by Macmillan, and *The Writer's and Artist's Yearbook*, published by A & C Black. These each give information on poetry, with specialist articles included on small presses and specialist magazines. Here you will find addresses, editors' names, short accounts of the preferences of the larger publishers, and also details of poetry associations and cooperatives.

Magazines

In recent years, there has been a noticeable increase in magazines about writing, with articles by seasoned professionals on all aspects of writing, including market information, research, up-dates on publishers and so on. The most comprehensive and easily available is *Writing Magazine* which is stocked at W.H. Smith. But there are others, some of them produced by writing groups with diverse interests. The most well-known are:

Freelance Writing and Photography, Tregeraint House, Zennor, St. Ives, Cornwall TR26 3DB.
Quartos, BCM Writer, 27 Old Gloucester Street, London WC1N 3XX.
Writers News, PO Box 4, Nairn, Scotland IV12 4HU.

Arts associations

Details and addresses, with the names of Arts and literature officers, are all in the two reference books. They publish magazines and diaries of events with promotional material. For instance, in the Yorkshire and North Lincolnshire area the Yorkshire and Humberside Arts prints a magazine called *Artscene* which lists events for each month, with commentary and reviews, and includes a list of local contacts for each variety of artistic activity.

Professional associations
Again, these are listed in the reference books, but special mention should be made of these two national groups:

The Poetry Society
The Poetry Society has been in existence since 1909 and is the central organisation in English poetry. It can offer members general information, a quarterly magazine, *Poetry Review*, an advice and information service and a critical service. This last item runs on the principle that for a small sum, you receive a professional critique of your work. The address is: 22 Betterton Street, London WC2H 9BU.

The National Convention of Poets and Small Presses
The National Convention has to be the best event in which to make contacts and network both yourself and your poetry. The event lasts for a weekend, and the staple of this is a series of readings. But if you are serious about promoting your poetry and you want to meet most of the people whose names you have seen in the poetry pages of the reference books, go to this. The address is: Scratch, 9 Chestnut Road, Eaglescliffe, Stockton-on-Tees TS16 0AB.

Question
Do people respect a poet who has published his or her work with self-finance?

Answer
Yes, if the writing is good enough! If you are convinced that you have something to say to your contemporaries, then this method ensures that at least some of them become aware of what you want to say and how you say it.

DEFINING THE REWARDS

No matter which option you choose in terms of publishing, promoting and advertising your poetry, all these strategies are well-established. Many successful poets have arrived at a position of high esteem by self-publishing in the first place. The hard fact is that large companies such as Faber, Oxford or Chatto are inundated with submissions. The policy at Oxford University Press, for instance, is to choose just one new poet to publish each year. They prefer to publish established names because they can virtually ensure a certain sales figure.

So what are your rewards for all this energy and commitment? They could be summarised like this:

- personal satisfaction: seeing your work in print
- responses from colleagues, peers, professionals
- critical responses – objectively done, by strangers!
- the verification that you have something to communicate.

There is an element of *catharsis* in writing poetry – a release of strong feelings, an inward soul-searching if you like. Poetry deals in feelings as well as thoughts. It is not the same as philosophy and a poet needs to think that some of his own emotional responses to human experience have been communicated to others.

CASE STUDIES

Paul goes it alone

Paul was fresh from sixth form college and had decided to take a year out before going on to university. Since his first 'A' level English classes, he had been excited by the idea, as well as the actual production of poetry. The idea of being a poet was a dramatic concept. As he had also studied drama, the two went together well.

When most of his friends were joining bands and learning the guitar, Paul decided to do more than simply write poetry – he also wanted to be a personality. He would give performances of poetry and bring it to life. His English teacher told him that very few aspiring writers ever made it to the privileged position of being able to spend all day 'being a professional poet'. But Paul had seen the best – Roger McGough, Brian Patten, Ian McMillan and others, and was aware that radio and television were opening out and being receptive to poetry as never before.

He worked hard during his year out learning the skills by doing readings whenever and wherever he could. He promoted himself in local newspapers – including the free ones. He acted as if he were a published poet. In fact, he had six poems printed in the college magazine, but teachers had said that he had real talent. Confidence was not a problem.

Paul did well. He was definitely noticed. A part-time arts organiser for his town approached him with a plan to put together an anthology of local writing, and to hold a small literature festival in the summer. His musician friends were only too happy to take part as well. It all proved to him that you need to be seen and heard as often as possible in the poetry scene.

Jane does some teamwork

Jane and her friends were housewives with a passion for poems and stories. They had been going to classes for literature for about three years and had started a part-time degree. They went to every literary event they could and finally started writing themselves. They had come across Pam Ayre's poetry and realised that you could write poems about teeth and dentists, not just red roses and loved ones. Jane wanted to write funny poetry – and she and her friends looked into the possibility of a book.

A local printing company gave them an estimate, but it was too expensive, even if all four of them shared the cost. They sorted out their best ten poems, then took the 40, with some drawings, to the local college. A project was born. Six months later, three art students had produced covers and layout, laminated the book, and all that was left was promotion and readings.

Jane's name, along with her friends, was on the cover, and it was a real success story. They were soon in demand as an 'act' at everything from Women's Institute gatherings to the writers' circle and local radio event-spots.

Not many writers would have realised that starting off with a joint-publication is a cheap but effective option, and means that you share not only the cost but the responsibility involved when you work with others and start to create 'a public' for your work. Jane had seen instinctively that reticence was an enemy to success and that teamwork was the best way to advance.

DISCUSSION POINTS

1. What are the advantages of being in a writers' directory if you don't want to perform or read your work in public?

2. Suggest some methods of promoting your poetry to the BBC. You want your poetry to be included in a radio programme. What is the procedure?

Glossary

Assonance A type of half-rhyme, often using similar vowel-sounds, as in rhymes with stain/stone or hole/heal.

Alliteration A cluster of consonants. 'The shiny snow slewed down'.

Anapaest A stress pattern having two unstressed followed by one stress syllable, *eg - -/*. The word *serenade* illustrates this.

Bathos Writing which changes mood or subject sharply from 'sublime to ridiculous'. For instance: *He took with him his deepest thoughts, his honest reflections, and his underwear.*

Blank verse Another name for iambic pentameter. (see *metre*).

Caesura A pause or hiatus in the middle of a line.

Canon The term used to define the texts included in the accepted list of major authors in the study of literature.

Caricature An exaggerated description of the subject, as in political satire.

Cliché An over-used word or phrase, often having no real effect when used. Examples are: *At sixes and sevens, all at sea, one degree under etc.*

Colloquial Ordinary, everyday language (contrasted with literary diction).

Consonance This is a repetition of several consonants, but with vowels used in between: 'Out of this house – *said rider to reader'* (W.H. Auden).

Couplet Two lines in a poem, often rhymed.

Dactyl A metrical foot with the stress pattern /--.

Didactic Something that 'teaches' a lesson or a moral – setting out to inform.

Dimeter. A metrical foot having two syllables: *'Never, – While I – Stand here'.*

Elegy A poem praising or celebrating a subject, it laments a death or loss.

Enjambment The 'run on' from one line to the next without punctuation.

Epigram A short, witty saying, often about a person.

Free verse A technique that does not use set forms or metrical structures.

Haiku A short poem, Japanese in origin, having syllables in each line totalling 5/7/5.

Hexameter A metrical line with six feet (twelve syllables) for instance: *Threw forth most dainty odours, and most sweet delight* (Edmund Spenser (1552–99), from *The Garden of Adonis*).

Hymn A poem or song in praise of something – usually religious.

Iambic A two-stress metrical foot, with the pattern unstress-stress (-/) as in the word *unknown*.

Idiom This is used to refer to a style of writing following the language-use of a specific kind of form or convention, such as the idiom of working-class protest or of Romantic ballads *etc.*

Imagery The language used to express meanings which are not literally true.

Irony Expression having a 'surface' meaning which is the opposite of what is said.

Lyric poetry This refers to songs and poems that are not primarily narrative or dramatic. That is, a poem that describes or expresses thought and feeling.

Metaphor An imaginative way of writing, comparing two similar concepts or objects. *eg Loneliness is a cloak you wear* relates a mood to a particular object we can visualise.

Metre The rules, stemming from classical poetry, covering the metrical feet in formal poetry. In English, the four main metres are iambic: -/ trochaic:/- dactylic: /-- and anapaestic: --/. In lines, the commonest lengths are five feet (pentameter) and four feet (tetrameter).

Modernism The period roughly from 1890 to the 1920's in which much experimental poetry was written, thus revolutionising the approach to formal poetry and expanding the possibilities of free verse and poetic form.

Monologue A poem spoken by one imagined speaker. These may be comic as in music-hall recitations, or serious, as in Browning's *Men and Women* poems.

Ode In English poetry, an ode usually contains strong declarations and feeling about a person or object. The form is often in stanzas in particular style and metre.

Paradox A seeming contradiction in a statement: 'Happy sadness'.

Parody A 'spoof' – a copying or 'take-off' of a style, usually for comedy.

Pathos Strong, prominent expression of feeling.

Pentameter A metrical line of five feet (ten syllables): *Now is the winter of our discontent* (William Shakespeare, *Richard III*).

Personification An image that describes inanimate objects as if they were human or animal.

Poem A form of writing in which verbal combinations and succinct feeling mix in either metrical or free forms. The use of the word is complicated by the use of the word 'poetic' to describe any passionate or lyrical use of language, or even image.

Post-modern A word with several implications, but primarily referring to the current social conditions of rapid change and lack of stable artistic values. A cultural climate in which free expression and egalitarian concepts of art tend to dominate all forms.

Prosody The rules governing metrical shaping of poetry in rhymes and syllables.

Pun A play on words, giving a double meaning. For example – 'monks have dirty habits'.

Rhetoric The use of powerful, persuasive expression, as in speeches in politics.

Rhyme scheme A pattern of end-rhymes, noted by the use of capital letters for each set of lines that rhyme, as in AABB which would be two rhyming couplets.

Satire An attack on a subject by means of ridicule or abuse.

Simile A simple, direct comparison, such as 'He ran like the wind'. Similes use the words *like* and *as*.

Sonnet A lyric poem of 14 lines, with a specific rhyme scheme.

Stressed line A line using the same number of stressed syllables per line, but in random positions (often used by Philip Larkin).

Stanza A division of a poem; a section, often in a set number of lines.

Structure The way a poem is unified into a coherent whole as the feeling and thinking develop from A to Z.

Symbol An image that places one item for another, representing it totally by suggestion and the linking of a set of ideas and associations. As in the 'Red rose' of England or the 'White dove of peace'.

Tetrameter A metrical line having four feet (eight syllables) *eg Farewell sweet love, I lose you now.*

Trimeter A metrical line having three feet (six syllables) *eg The heart I have is yours.*

Tone The writer's attitude to the subject as conveyed by a cadence in the structures of the words and statements.

Trochee In metre, a foot with the stress pattern of: /-.

Verse The term verse is used in two ways (1) to differentiate the less intellectual and more accessible (often rhymed) writing in poetic form and (2) as a name for a section of a long poem.

Answers to Discussion Points

CHAPTER 1

1. You find feedback, critical response, opportunity for contacts *etc.*

2. Yes, if you are the type. Roger Woddis clearly was. It certainly helps if you have a sense of satire and a political or humorous flavour to your work.

CHAPTER 2

1. You need to find out quickly what sort of proportion of time poetry writing takes up. It is obvious that you need plenty of other poets around to learn from and exchange ideas with.

2. Date sent, where it was sent to and notes about previous responses.

CHAPTER 3

1. Check on whether there is a local or regional dialect society. These are listed under Professional organisations in the *Writers and Artists' Yearbook.*

2. No. There is no reason why it should be harder. The only factor worth mentioning here is that some magazines actively encourage metrical verse – notably *Literary Review* and *Orbis*. There are also competitions specifically for formal poetry, organised by these two publications. See the reference books.

CHAPTER 4

1. The techniques to work on are using adjectives and adverbs with a concrete sense. For instance, describe with words such as tawny brown rather than a vague, general colour.

2. Normally, rural topics, descriptive poems, but also symbolic poems conveying a mood.

CHAPTER 5

1. It is not possible for everyone, but if you have the temperament and the vigour in your words and structure, then learn by copying forms and uses of slang or idiom.

2. There are none. Rhyme can be used for any subject. However, it is clearly more of a personal challenge to use end-rhyme about a serious or solemn topic.

CHAPTER 6

1. Mainly, keep you name before the public eye. Offer to be involved in publicity schemes, be prominent in all artistic and literary events. Have your name and details in a directory of writers (see Chapter 10).

2. Do not tell them your life story. Do not write reams of information about the poems.

CHAPTER 7

1. For example: a reading, a quiz, a workshop for children, a community anthology.

2. By these methods: local news items, supermarket and post office announcements, flyers in shops and community centres *etc*

CHAPTER 8

1. You could not, from most books, but there is one outstanding exception – *Poet's Markets* (see Further Reading).

2. Work on two principles: balance long with short and narrative with lyrical. Mix, match and contrast.

CHAPTER 9

1. First, send a CV and a few examples of your work. Then apply to schemes for a grant or writers' bursary.

2. From local council funding, arts association grant or sponsorship from business.

CHAPTER 10

1. Not so many good reasons! But the important one is that your name is seen by others in the business.

2. The BBC has a firm policy here. Check in the *Writers and Artists' Yearbook* for the details of which person and department to send your work to, then send CV and samples.

Further Reading

REFERENCE BOOKS

The Writers' and Artists' Yearbook (A. & C. Black, annual).
The Writer's Handbook, Barry Turner (Macmillan, annual).
The Writer's Companion, Barry Turner (Macmillan 1995).
Poet's Market and *Writer's Market* from Writers Digest Books, annual. 38 Carver Road, London SE24 9LT.

GENERAL BOOKS ON WRITING

The Art of Writing, Geoffrey Ashe (Made Simple Books 1972).
Guide to Written English, James Aitchison (Cassell 1995).
Creative Writing, Julia Casterton (Macmillan 1986).
Creative Writing, Dianne Doubtfire (Hodder 1983, reprinted 1995).
Creative Writing, John Fairfax (Elm Tree 1989).

BOOKS ON WRITING POETRY

The Way to Write Poetry, Michael Baldwin (Elm Tree 1988).
Poetry Workbook, Eric Boagey (Unwin Hyman 1977).
The Craft of Writing Poetry, Alison Chisholm (Allison & Busby 1994).
Writing Poetry (with cassette), Doris Corti (Thomas & Lochar 1995).
How to Publish your Poetry, Peter Finch (Allison & Busby 1989).
Against the Grain, Ian Macmillan (Nelson 1989).
How to Enjoy Poetry, Vernon Scannell (Piatkus 1983).
The Poet's Manual, Frances Stillman (Thames & Hudson 1992).

MAGAZINES OF INTEREST TO POETS

Freelance Writing and Poetry, Tregeraint House, Zennor, St. Ives, Cornwall TR26 3DB.

Quartos, BCM Writer, 27 Old Gloucester Street, London WC1N 3XX.

Writers News, PO Box 4, Nairn, Scotland IV12 4HU.

Writing Magazine, PO Box 4, Nairn, Scotland IV12 4HU.

THE ESTABLISHED MAGAZINES

Acumen, 6 The Mount, Higher Furzeham, Brixham, Devon TQ5 8QY.

Agenda, 5 Cranbourne Court, Albert Bridge Road, London SW11 4PE.

Chapman, 4 Broughton Place, Edinburgh EH1 3RX.

Critical Quarterly, University of Strathclyde, Glasgow G1 1XH.

The Literary Review, 51 Beak Street, London W1R 3LF.

London Magazine, 30 Thurloe Place, London SW7 2HQ.

Orbis, 199 Long Shoot, Nuneaton, Worcestershire CV11 6JQ.

Pennine Platform, Ingmanthorpe Hall Farm Cottage, Wetherby, West Yorkshire W22 5EQ.

Poetry Review, The Poetry Society, 22 Betterton Street, London SW7 2HQ.

Stand Magazine, 179 Wingrove Road, Newcastle upon Tyne, NE4 9DA.

Staple, Tor Cottage, 81 Cavendish Road, Matlock, Derbyshire DE4 3HD.

Useful Addresses

ORGANISATIONS OF INTEREST TO POETS

Apples and Snakes, Unit A11, Hatcham Mews Business Centre, Hatcham Mews Park, London SE14 5QA.

Castle of Dreams Writers' Co-operative, Pease Street, Darlington DL1 4EU.

The International Society of Poets, Dept 9002, Freepost, London 2229, London EC1B 1TY.

National Poetry Foundation, 27 Mill Road, Fareham, Hampshire PO16 0TH.

The Poetry Business, The Studio, Byrom Arcade, Huddersfield HD1 1ND.

WRITING COURSES: A SELECTION

Arvon Foundation, Lumb Bank, Hebden Bridge HX7 6DF.

Creative Arts Courses, The Indian King Arts Centre, Fore St, Camelford, Cornwall PL32 9PG.

Pembrokeshire Retreat, Rhosygilwen Mansion, Rhoshill, Nr. Cardigan, Dyfed.

Ty Newydd Writing Courses, Ty Newydd Llanysttumdwy, Cricieth, Gwyneth LL52 0LW.

University of Edinburgh, Centre for Continuing Education, Freepost EH 3376, 11 Buccleuch Place, Edinburgh EH8 9LW.

The Writers' College, Freepost PEG 1094, 7 Dale Street, Manchester M1 8DJ.

Index

CREATIVE WRITING
How to develop your writing skills for successful fiction and non-fiction work

Adèle Ramet

The term 'Creative Writing' covers a broad spectrum of skills from writing non-fiction articles and features for specialist magazines to romantic fiction, ghost stories and crime novels. This book guides you through key techniques, with exercises aimed at helping you to write more effectively in your chosen genre. You will be encouraged to approach your work from different angles, demonstrating how to bring a fresh slant to non-fiction pieces and how to involve yourself more fully in the lives of your fictional characters. Whatever your writing interest, this book will help you write more creatively and lead you further along the route towards publication. Adèle Ramet is Chairman of the South Eastern Writers Association and an experienced writing tutor. She has contributed widely to *Bella*, *Woman's Realm*, and many other leading women's magazines.

136pp. illus. 1 85703 451 1.

COPYRIGHT & LAW FOR WRITERS
How to protect yourself and your creative work

Helen Shay

This book will be a useful tool for any writer, but especially invaluable to beginners and those just starting to enjoy some success. Make sure you never receive any legal short change. This book takes you through the main legal implications relevant to writers, from first putting pen to paper/finger to keyboard through to selling work, entering a contract and onto collecting the full financial rewards due to you. It also explains exactly what to do if things go wrong. It explains the various pitfalls and how to steer clear of them – for example copyright infringement – whilst showing how to preserve your own rights, and learning how to publish and not be damned. A graduate of Manchester University, Helen Shay is a qualified solicitor of twelve years' standing. Currently working in an ombudsman's office in London, she is well-versed in the problems which can confront the individual versus large organisations. She also tutors and lectures part-time in business law. She is a member of the Society of Women Writers and Journalists and the Women Writers Network, and currently writes a regular legal column for *Writers News*.

96pp. illus. 1 85703 416 3.

STARTING TO WRITE
How to create written work for publication and profit

Marina & Deborah Oliver

How does a writer get started? How do writers manage the physical aspects? This new book shows would-be writers how to look at their motives, how to set realistic objectives, and how to devise a plan of action without wasting time and resources. Illustrated throughout with case studies, it will show you how to explore various options, discover what methods work best for you, and take advantage of tips from experienced writers. Start now, and learn how to get your work into print. Marina Oliver has written and published over 30 novels, published her own magazine, written and edited many booklets, and taught creative writing. Deborah Oliver has edited a monthly magazine and is currently production editor of a computer magazine.

124pp. illus. 1 85703 401 5.

HOW TO WRITE FOR PUBLICATION
Your practical guide to success

Chriss McCallum

'How can I sell my work? How do I protect my copyright? Can a magazine steal my story? Why just a printed rejection slip – can't editors tell me where I'm going wrong? Are writing courses worth the money? Should I get an agent?' Highly expert and practical, **How to Write for Publication** gives the often surprising answers to these and hundreds of other questions most often asked by the great silent majority of struggling writers, whether of fiction, nonfiction, poetry, drama, stories or articles. No author seriously interested in getting published can afford to be without this manual, packed with checklists, examples and key contacts. 'Handy for both professional and newcomer alike.' *Writers News*. 'Everything you ever wanted to know about the practical side of publishing . . . excellent.' *Competitors Journal*. 'Really definitive . . . Leaves every other similar book in its shade.' *Pause (National Poetry Foundation)*. Chriss McCallum has many years' experience as a professional Editor, and has worked for Collins, Penguin, W H Allen and other leading firms. She was publisher of *The Writers Voice* (1983-86) and is a Member of the Society of Authors, The Society of Women Writers & Journalists, and an Honorary Member of the Comedy Writers Association.

192pp. illus. 1 85703 140 7. 3rd edition.

How To Books

How To Books provide practical help on a large range of topics. They are available through all good bookshops or can be ordered direct from the distributors. Just tick the titles you want and complete the form on the following page.

___ Apply to an Industrial Tribunal (£7.99)
___ Applying for a Job (£7.99)
___ Applying for a United States Visa (£15.99)
___ Be a Freelance Journalist (£8.99)
___ Be a Freelance Secretary (£8.99)
___ Be a Local Councillor (£8.99)
___ Be an Effective School Governor (£9.99)
___ Become a Freelance Sales Agent (£9.99)
___ Become an Au Pair (£8.99)
___ Buy & Run a Shop (£8.99)
___ Buy & Run a Small Hotel (£8.99)
___ Cash from your Computer (£9.99)
___ Career Planning for Women (£8.99)
___ Choosing a Nursing Home (£8.99)
___ Claim State Benefits (£9.99)
___ Communicate at Work (£7.99)
___ Conduct Staff Appraisals (£7.99)
___ Conducting Effective Interviews (£8.99)
___ Copyright & Law for Writers (£8.99)
___ Counsel People at Work (£7.99)
___ Creating a Twist in the Tale (£8.99)
___ Creative Writing (£9.99)
___ Critical Thinking for Students (£8.99)
___ Do Voluntary Work Abroad (£8.99)
___ Do Your Own Advertising (£8.99)
___ Do Your Own PR (£8.99)
___ Doing Business Abroad (£9.99)
___ Emigrate (£9.99)
___ Employ & Manage Staff (£8.99)
___ Find Temporary Work Abroad (£8.99)
___ Finding a Job in Canada (£9.99)
___ Finding a Job in Computers (£8.99)
___ Finding a Job in New Zealand (£9.99)
___ Finding a Job with a Future (£8.99)
___ Finding Work Overseas (£9.99)
___ Freelance DJ-ing (£8.99)
___ Get a Job Abroad (£10.99)
___ Get a Job in America (£9.99)
___ Get a Job in Australia (£9.99)
___ Get a Job in Europe (£9.99)
___ Get a Job in France (£9.99)
___ Get a Job in Germany (£9.99)
___ Get a Job in Hotels and Catering (£8.99)
___ Get a Job in Travel & Tourism (£8.99)
___ Get into Films & TV (£8.99)
___ Get into Radio (£8.99)
___ Get That Job (£6.99)
___ Getting your First Job (£8.99)
___ Going to University (£8.99)
___ Helping your Child to Read (£8.99)
___ Investing in People (£8.99)
___ Invest in Stocks & Shares (£8.99)

___ Keep Business Accounts (£7.99)
___ Know Your Rights at Work (£8.99)
___ Know Your Rights: Teachers (£6.99)
___ Live & Work in America (£9.99)
___ Live & Work in Australia (£12.99)
___ Live & Work in Germany (£9.99)
___ Live & Work in Greece (£9.99)
___ Live & Work in Italy (£8.99)
___ Live & Work in New Zealand (£9.99)
___ Live & Work in Portugal (£9.99)
___ Live & Work in Spain (£7.99)
___ Live & Work in the Gulf (£9.99)
___ Living & Working in Britain (£8.99)
___ Living & Working in China (£9.99)
___ Living & Working in Hong Kong (£10.99)
___ Living & Working in Israel (£10.99)
___ Living & Working in Japan (£8.99)
___ Living & Working in Saudi Arabia (£12.99)
___ Living & Working in the Netherlands (£9.99)
___ Lose Weight & Keep Fit (£6.99)
___ Make a Wedding Speech (£7.99)
___ Making a Complaint (£8.99)
___ Manage a Sales Team (£8.99)
___ Manage an Office (£8.99)
___ Manage Computers at Work (£8.99)
___ Manage People at Work (£8.99)
___ Manage Your Career (£8.99)
___ Managing Budgets & Cash Flows (£9.99)
___ Managing Meetings (£8.99)
___ Managing Your Personal Finances (£8.99)
___ Market Yourself (£8.99)
___ Master Book-Keeping (£8.99)
___ Mastering Business English (£8.99)
___ Master GCSE Accounts (£8.99)
___ Master Languages (£8.99)
___ Master Public Speaking (£8.99)
___ Obtaining Visas & Work Permits (£9.99)
___ Organising Effective Training (£9.99)
___ Pass Exams Without Anxiety (£7.99)
___ Pass That Interview (£6.99)
___ Plan a Wedding (£7.99)
___ Prepare a Business Plan (£8.99)
___ Publish a Book (£9.99)
___ Publish a Newsletter (£9.99)
___ Raise Funds & Sponsorship (£7.99)
___ Rent & Buy Property in France (£9.99)
___ Rent & Buy Property in Italy (£9.99)
___ Retire Abroad (£8.99)
___ Return to Work (£7.99)
___ Run a Local Campaign (£6.99)
___ Run a Voluntary Group (£8.99)
___ Sell Your Business (£9.99)

How To Books

___ Selling into Japan (£14.99)	___ Use the Internet (£9.99)
___ Setting up Home in Florida (£9.99)	___ Winning Consumer Competitions (£8.99)
___ Spend a Year Abroad (£8.99)	___ Winning Presentations (£8.99)
___ Start a Business from Home (£7.99)	___ Work from Home (£8.99)
___ Start a New Career (£6.99)	___ Work in an Office (£7.99)
___ Starting to Manage (£8.99)	___ Work in Retail (£8.99)
___ Starting to Write (£8.99)	___ Work with Dogs (£8.99)
___ Start Word Processing (£8.99)	___ Working Abroad (£14.99)
___ Start Your Own Business (£8.99)	___ Working as a Holiday Rep (£9.99)
___ Study Abroad (£8.99)	___ Working in Japan (£10.99)
___ Study & Learn (£7.99)	___ Working in Photography (£8.99)
___ Study & Live in Britain (£7.99)	___ Working in the Gulf (£10.99)
___ Studying at University (£8.99)	___ Working on Contract Worldwide (£9.99)
___ Studying for a Degree (£8.99)	___ Working on Cruise Ships (£9.99)
___ Successful Grandparenting (£8.99)	___ Write a CV that Works (£7.99)
___ Successful Mail Order Marketing (£9.99)	___ Write a Press Release (£9.99)
___ Successful Single Parenting (£8.99)	___ Write a Report (£8.99)
___ Survive at College (£4.99)	___ Write an Assignment (£8.99)
___ Survive Divorce (£8.99)	___ Write an Essay (£7.99)
___ Surviving Redundancy (£8.99)	___ Write & Sell Computer Software (£9.99)
___ Take Care of Your Heart (£5.99)	___ Write Business Letters (£8.99)
___ Taking in Students (£8.99)	___ Write for Publication (£8.99)
___ Taking on Staff (£8.99)	___ Write for Television (£8.99)
___ Taking Your A-Levels (£8.99)	___ Write Your Dissertation (£8.99)
___ Teach Abroad (£8.99)	___ Writing a Non Fiction Book (£8.99)
___ Teach Adults (£8.99)	___ Writing & Selling a Novel (£8.99)
___ Teaching Someone to Drive (£8.99)	___ Writing & Selling Short Stories (£8.99)
___ Travel Round the World (£8.99)	___ Writing Reviews (£8.99)
___ Use a Library (£6.99)	___ Your Own Business in Europe (£12.99)

To: Plymbridge Distributors Ltd, Plymbridge House, Estover Road, Plymouth PL6 7PZ.
Customer Services Tel: (01752) 202301. Fax: (01752) 202331.

Please send me copies of the titles I have indicated. Please add postage & packing
(UK £1, Europe including Eire, £2, World £3 airmail).

☐ I enclose cheque/PO payable to Plymbridge Distributors Ltd for £ _____

☐ Please charge to my ☐ MasterCard, ☐ Visa, ☐ AMEX card.

Account No. ☐☐☐☐☐☐☐☐☐☐☐☐☐☐☐☐

Card Expiry Date ☐ ☐ 19 ☎ **Credit Card orders may be faxed or phoned.**

Customer Name (CAPITALS) ....

Address ....

.... Postcode ....

Telephone .... Signature ....

Every effort will be made to despatch your copy as soon as possible but to avoid possible
disappointment please allow up to 21 days for despatch time (42 days if overseas). Prices
and availability are subject to change without notice.

Code BPA